Professional Counseling 101

Building a Strong Professional Identity

by Mark Pope

AMERICAN COUNSELING ASSOCIATION
5999 Stevenson Avenue
Alexandria, VA 22304
www.counseling.org

Professional
Counseling 101

Building a
Strong
Professional
Identity

10 9 8 7 6 5 4 3 2 1

American Counseling Association
5999 Stevenson Avenue
Alexandria, VA 22304

Director of Publications
Carolyn C. Baker

Production Manager
Bonny E. Gaston

Cover and text design by Bonny E. Gaston.

Library of Congress Cataloging-in-Publication Data
Pope, Mark, 1952–
Professional counseling 101 : building a strong professional identity / Mark Pope.
p. cm.
ISBN 1-55620-259-8 (alk. paper)
1. Counseling. I. Title: Professional counseling one hundred
one.   II. Title: Professional counseling one hundred and one. III. Title.

BF637.C6P592 2005
158´.3—dc22   2005025159

Contents

Foreword
(or Forward!)

Most presidents of organizations work hard and are hardly remembered for more than a few years. Fortunately there are some exceptions. Mark Pope is a president who deserves to be remembered. This book is a compilation of the essays that he wrote for *Counseling Today* when he was President of the American Counseling Association.

These essays are easy to understand and yet contain some complicated topics. I am reminded of Enrique Jardiel Poncela's statement, "When something can be read without effort, great effort has gone into its writing." You can feel his effort and compassion.

Each of the essays has a powerful message about organizations, justice, culture, and professional identity. Collectively the essays provide the reader with an opportunity to feel what the world is like for an exceptional professional counselor. The reader will quickly understand that Mark was not born with a silver spoon in his mouth nor did he rise in the counseling profession because he went along with whoever could help him with his agendas. Mark Pope is a unique individual who not only lives his principles but actually wears them on the outside for everyone to see.

I especially appreciate the opening chapters about Mark Pope the person and his view of professional counseling. By sharing his own grief as he pays homage to my colleague Mary Arnold, he models for all of us how we deal with the pain and suffering of our work. The reader will feel his deep compassion and caring for others.

These essays will be of value for the counselor-in-training as well as the practicing professional counselor. Each essay seems to force the reader to wrestle with a different aspect of his or her professional identity. May you grow and profit personally and professionally from "Pope 101."

As Will Rogers said, "We can't all be heroes, because somebody has to sit on the curb and clap as they go by."

With a loud applause,

—Jon Carlson, PsyD, EdD
Distinguished Professor
Governors State University

About the Author

Mark Pope, EdD, is a professor in the Division of Counseling and Family Therapy at the University of Missouri–Saint Louis. His many books, journal articles, book chapters, and presentations to professional groups focus on career counseling and multicultural counseling and their intersection. He has served as President of the American Counseling Association, the National Career Development Association, and the Association for Gay, Lesbian, and Bisexual Issues in Counseling.

He has written on the career development of ethnic, racial, and sexual minorities; the history of and public policy issues in counseling; psychological testing; violence in schools; international issues in counseling; and the teaching of career counseling. His work is published as books and book chapters, as conference presentations, and in such journals as the *Journal of Counseling & Development*, *The Career Development Quarterly*, *The Family Journal*, *Journal of Multicultural Counseling and Development*, *Journal of Vocational Behavior*, *Journal of Career Development*, and *The Counseling Psychologist*.

He has been the editor of *The Career Development Quarterly* and served on the editorial boards of and as a reviewer for that journal as well as the *Journal of Counseling & Development*, *The Family Journal*, and *Developmental Psychology*. He edited two special sections of *The Career Development Quarterly*: *Challenges for Career Counseling in Asia* (2002, with Fred Leong) and *Gay/Lesbian Career Development* (1995).

He edited *The Career Counseling Casebook: A Resource for Practitioners, Students, and Counselor Educators* (2002, with Spencer Niles and Jane Goodman) and two volumes of *Experiential Activities for Teaching Career Counseling Classes and Facilitating Career Groups* (2000 and 2005, with Carole Minor) for which he received an NCDA Presidential Recognition Award in 2003. He is the founding editor (with Martha Russell) of *Global Career Resources*, an international newsletter for career counseling and organization development, which has been published continuously since 1995.

In 2001, he received the Robert Swan Lifetime Achievement Award for Career Development from the California Career Development Association as well as the Kitty Cole Human Rights Award from the American Counseling Association. He is a Fellow of the National Career Development Association, American Psychological Association, Society of Counseling Psychology (APA Division 17), and Society for the Psychological Study of Lesbian and Gay Issues (APA Division 44).

Part I

Introduction

Chapter 1

Introduction to Our Profession (or Why Are We Here?)

Welcome! This book is about the profession of counseling. It's kind of like your personal guide to our profession (yes, you're one of us now). In these pages you will learn about the history of our little (and growing) band of sisters and brothers. You will learn about what makes us different from clinical psychologists and social workers. You will learn to appreciate diversity in all its many hues. You will learn to be proud of the work that we do in the world. All of this in one little book. Amazing!

You know, this could turn your world around.

Most of these essays were originally published in *Counseling Today* as my column when I was ACA President—from July 2003 to June 2004. Hey, if you kept those *CT*s, you might not even need this book, except that there are some other essays on history and strangers on the road and a special exhortation on licensing, certification, accreditation, and ethics (nice word, *exhortation*). So, it's probably worth it to spend the money and buy the book. Anyway, there might be a hidden treasure or two that you missed the first time around.

If you're a newbie counselor-in-training, I hope you like this book. The essays were truly a labor of love, but they were written for all of us in professional counseling. Whether you are a first semester master's student in the Introduction to Counseling course or you are a wizened old veteran of the professional counseling wars, this book is for you.

This little book is written in an easily accessible style. Please, please, do not use it as the blueprint for a paper in your Theories of Counseling class. It's not in APA publication style, because it's not supposed to be. It's different. It's more in a conversational style. Me talking to you personally, one-on-one about our profession.

Above all else, I hope the book makes you feel something, and I hope you love (or discover that you love) this work as much as I do!

—Warmly,
Mark

Chapter 2

Meet Mark Pope

A s I sit here musing over my first column as ACA President, I wonder how you perceive me. Now, I know that "you" don't perceive me at all. There is no universal "you"; there is only a whole bunch of individual "you's." I also understand that there are some of you who don't really care who is our President, and (for your information) I don't take it personally at all. (Smile.) I know that's just the way it is. But I thought if I wrote a very personal column to begin my term, you might begin to care. I know from the career research that many of you are more feeling-oriented characterologically and that this type of approach will be more appealing to you. It's good to begin your term broadly appealing to a large majority of your constituents, colleagues, friends, and family (work from least appealing term to most appealing term). Many of you don't know me, but I plan to fix that with this column.

I was born a poor, gay, Cherokee boy in rural southeast Missouri. (This has possibilities for a book or maybe even a movie, eh?) I wear each of those descriptors like a badge of courage. I am proud of who I am, proud of each of those various facets of my personal cultural identity. I figure it is better than hating yourself.

I have a rather dry sense of humor. This was pointed out to me when I was in college by Charles Claiborn (now at Arizona State University and a past-editor of our *Journal of Counseling & Development*), but he was my classmate and friend and "Chuck" to me. He said he loved my sense of humor. Unbeknownst (nice word, especially when you see it) to me, I was an unconscious comedian. When I first knew Chuck, I was an upperclass student at the University of Missouri–Columbia (read "conservative, agrarian, Midwestern"), and I had long hair down to my shoulders, wire-rimmed glasses, a Navy peacoat, and short beard, and wore a "McGovern for President" button. We were giving tours in 1972 of the university to new freshmen and their parents as part of the Freshman Summer Orientation Program. I believe that the explicit goal of the university's summer orientation program was to calm the fears of the parents about little Johnny from Fisk, Missouri, going off to the big university and changing—like maybe becoming a Marxist or lesbian or . . . well, you get the picture. Irony is defined as "incongruity between the actual result of a sequence of events and the normal or expected result." I hope that you are enjoying this.

I have "interesting" ancestors. One of my grandfathers was a Baptist minister and one was a "bootlegger." For those of you who are unfamiliar with these terms, a minister is a religious leader who has been given the license to officiate at Protestant church worship. You might have known that, but bootlegger is a more esoteric word with roots in the Prohibition era and the various mountain ranges of the Mid-South (Ozark, Appalachian, Blue Ridge, etc.) that provided a home for many of my relatives. A bootlegger is one who manufactures, sells, or transports for sale adult beverages, usually containing alcohol, and contrary to law. The most important piece of that is the last phrase, "contrary to law." Are you beginning to care yet?

My family has unusual names. Remember that I grew up in a predominant French and Cherokee area of the country (southeast Missouri). As a direct result of that, my family has unusual names (for which I blame, as well as all adolescent trauma, on my mother). Like my brothers' names, Isom and Dolen, or my mother Ethyle (pronounced "ee-thil"). Or my "real" name—Markel LaVern Pope, which I quickly shortened during *early* adolescence to "Mark." Are you caring yet?

See, the bottomline for me is that I want every one of you in our profession to care. Not necessarily about me, although that would be okay too, but most importantly about our profession. I want you to care deeply and passionately. Really, I do. Because that is how I feel and why I have devoted, am devoting, and will continue to devote substantial portions of life, time, energy, and financial resources to our profession. Someone once said to me that "money is congealed consciousness," so where you put your money is about what you value, what is important to you in your life. Here's another image: spending money is like voting, like casting your ballot for what is important to you. I'm glad that you have chosen to value our profession and what we do every day by joining and rejoining your professional association—ACA.

Now, if everything has worked, you are really caring. And that is what we need. We need every one of you to care in order to actually accomplish the important tasks ahead for our profession.

Note: This chapter was originally published as the "ACA President's Column" in the July 2003 issue of *Counseling Today*. It was my first column as ACA President.

Part II

Professional Identity Development

Chapter 3

Ich Bien Ein
Professional Counselor

With apologies to President John Kennedy, it's a good powerful statement. If this were Jeopardy (the television game show), the correct response would be "who are we?" A question to be asked regularly even if (and especially when) you are sure you really know the answer. Now, you'd think that by the time you are 51 (both me and ACA) or over 100 (in actual ancestral years, through career counseling and the National Career Development Association), that you'd know, but sometimes I forget that we are still "in process." We are a process-oriented profession. We learn process, process, process. It is drummed into our heads in our graduate training. Those of us who are too outcome oriented (and you know who you are) are regularly confronted by such phrases as "too problem solving, too early." In counselor education one of the prime commandments is "thou (Old English for "you") shalt (Old English for "should") not problem solve." Our role is to help the client discover and use their own process. They have to learn, and we are the facilitators of their learning. It's more important to teach a process than to give them an answer. ("Give a person a fish and they will eat for a day. Teach a person to fish . . .") Okay, I give up. Their clichés have trumped my clichés. I accept this "truth."

Now back to this identity query: Who are we? What makes us different from psychiatrists, psychologists of all stripes (counseling, clinical, school, etc.), social workers (clinical or otherwise), or couples/marriage/family therapists? What makes a professional school counselor different from a teacher? What makes a career counselor different from a career coach? We (and I) have to be able to answer such questions for a whole host of reasons. We have to be able to differentiate ourselves from these other professions so that we can answer the question: Why do we exist? (too Cartesian, I fear, but nonetheless important). Even the Rand Corporation asked that question recently of me when they visited ACA headquarters in their preparation of a Congressional report on TRICARE reimbursement for professional counselors.

To answer the question, you have to first know where we come from. (I'll try not to be boring.) Our roots are in a variety of other professions and include the social work profession, applied psychology, assessment, humanism/progressivism, multiculturalism, medicine, and education. But we have grown and developed over the last 100 years and are now so much more than just our initial parts.

Traditional social work is focused on "case management" not counseling. Those in the "mental health specialization" of social work are trained in the clinical aspects, but almost 90% of the other social workers are policy and case management focused and their respective internships, while thorough, are not counseling focused.

Our psychological ancestors have taken a more medical focus in their work. Even the counseling psychologists have abandoned the K–12 schools (not all) and a more traditional developmental and preventive focus. Some still mouth the words of primary prevention, but it is sometimes hard to tell a Clinical from a Counseling Psychologist these days.

Humanism and its political reflection Progressivism are waning. Evidence: (1) the virtual demise of one of our founding Divisions—the Counseling Association for Humanistic Education and Development (C-AHEAD) (JOIN NOW!) and (2) the rise of fundamentalist strains of religion around our Earth (whether they are Islamic or Jewish or Christian).

Anyway . . .

Why am I, the President of ACA, asking such a question? Let me tell you. (You knew that was coming.)

I have just returned from the Carter Center's Annual Mental Health Symposium in Atlanta where all of the mental "health" organizations in the US gathered to discuss the implementation of the report of President George W. Bush's New Freedom Commission on Mental Health. Twenty five years ago a similar commission was initiated by President Jimmy Carter and its report led to the demise of residential treatment of the mentally ill and to the rise of the community mental health movement.

I have not been around a lot of psychiatrists recently (I had enough of them in my early career in psychiatric hospitals and drug abuse treatment) until this meeting. First, you should know that I do not tolerate arrogance easily. I had forgotten how wonderful psychotropic medications are and how everything can be fixed by such pills. Not. I had forgotten how much verbal and behavioral therapies are valued by this group. Not. And I had forgotten how much psychiatrists are valued by the other medical specialties, such as surgery and oncology. Double not. Remember that psychiatry is looked down upon (by the hard science medical faction) as a "soft" or "fuzzy" part of medicine. Remember also that medical schools have a strongly hierarchical and patriarchal structure and that psychiatrists are trained in medical schools. (You knew that, just wanted to remind you.)

It was quite entertaining and eye opening. I realized (once again) why I strongly identify as a professional counselor. I'm pretty sure that everyone who is a professional counselor should have this experience at least once in their lifetime, as it made me appreciate what we bring to the whole mental health equation in the world, why we are unique, and our reason for existence. (I'm getting to that, but I want to build the tension.)

Okay, here's my take on who we are. We are the developmentalists who focus on the life transitions of people. While many of our mental health colleagues are focusing on illness, we are focusing on health, wellness, growth, development, and prevention. Insurance companies don't much like such language, as they are focused on making a profit for their shareholders and feel that prevention costs money upfront and affects this year's annual report. This short-sighted belief is what drives mental "illness" models and traditional Western symptomatic medicine approaches. It keeps us all trapped.

Fortunately, much of what was presented at the Carter Center Mental Health Symposium was focused on what our profession knows and does every day. Here are some of those new-to-them truths uncovered by researchers and presented to the very astute and attentive audience at this national symposium:

1. The big three in mental health recovery are prevention, early diagnosis, and treatment. (Thank you.)
2. Suicide is the leading cause of violent deaths in the world (suicide 49%, homicide 32%, war 19%).
3. Of those with diagnosable mental disorders, only half get some treatment.
4. The most serious of the mental disorders begin in childhood and adolescence. Note that 15 is the age of onset in 50% of those who are diagnosed with anxiety disorders. This is a worldwide statistic.
5. Poverty has a strong relationship to mental illness.
6. Collaborative care models (integrated care where we all work together) have been shown to dramatically improve the treatment of mental health disorders (but this is always the first model to *not* be implemented—usually for cost reasons and not for efficacy, obviously).
7. We cannot reach children and adolescents through mental health clinics and hospitals. The primary gathering place for children and adolescents is the schools (followed closely by shopping malls—smile).
8. Even if there are genes for depression or chemicals to relieve symptoms, those who have them will still need psychosocial supportive therapies to survive the experience and relearn developmentally appropriate, healthy behaviors so that they can achieve recovery and true mental health.

This statement was made on various occasions: "Mental health is more than the lack of mental illness." (Thank you.) Even if you identify a pathogen (genetic, hormonal, chemical imbalance) and you eliminate or correct it, what is left? Such simple elimination does not assure full recovery, as there will generally remain behavioral/developmental deficits. You must acknowledge that developmental anomalies persist, that the learned compensatory behavior does not just simply correct itself. Sometimes, yes, with time and a healthy environment, but rarely. The old behaviors learned to cope with the pathogen will not just evaporate; nature abhors a vacuum. Alleviation of symptoms and elimination of the pathogen is the foundation upon which health is built, but it is not sufficient in and of itself to assure true mental health.

The Commission on Mental Health had some recommendations that I think most of us will applaud vigorously. Here's a few for your delight:

1. Abandon the language of stigma and embrace a recovery and resilience paradigm.
2. Normalize mental health treatment.
3. Individualize mental health treament.
4. Inform other mental health professions about what each does and then integrate service delivery as well as professional literatures.
5. Teach young people about differences.
6. Use strength-based rather than deficit-based language.
7. Use the school-based mental heath practitioners (school counselors, school social workers, school psychologists) to provide screening, assessment, treatment, and referral.
8. Integrate the delivery of mental health services throughout the various institutions of the community.

So I want to thank President Bush and Mrs. Carter. It was a delightful event. One that I hope ACA and our Divisions will attend regularly. Gail Adams, AMHCA President, and I sat together and were constantly whispering back and forth to each other about how we wished that ASCA and ACCA and NCDA and others were here. We cannot afford to have mental health relegated to the mental illness people, as Dr. William Glasser continues to remind us.

I'm just glad I have professional counseling training and I'm just glad for our strong professional identity. I am thankful every day that I have found our profession and that we exist. I sometimes think that we are the only hope for the world. I guess I'm just a professional counseling fanatic who believes passionately in who we are and what we do. (It's the least you could expect from an ACA President.) Thanks to each of you. I really do love our profession. Big hug!

Note: This chapter was originally published as the "ACA President's Column" in the January 2004 issue of *Counseling Today*.

Chapter 4

Your Professional Responsibility: It's a Good Thing

I bet when you read the title to my column this time you thought, "He's either going to lecture us today about what we ought to be doing or this is going to be an homage to Martha Stewart." And, if you selected the former, you'd be right (again). But as ACA President, your President, it's my job and I take it seriously. Anyway, my Mom did it to me. I get to do it to you. It's a circle of life thing.

I'm probably preaching to the proverbial choir here. You already belong to the American Counseling Association or you probably wouldn't be reading this column right now. But there are a whole bunch of us out there who don't belong (yet). The good news is, according to the latest *Occupational Outlook Handbook,* there are some 465,000 professional counselors just in the USA, with 205,000 who specialize in educational, vocational, and school counseling; 110,000 in rehabilitation counseling; 67,000 in mental health counseling; 61,000 in substance abuse and behavioral disorder counseling; and 21,000 in marriage, couple, and family counseling. The bad news is there are only 50,000 members of ACA. Now, that's not all bad, but it's simply not good enough.

Did you know that there is a direct relationship between your membership in ACA and your personal happiness? Yes, it is true. So, let me congratulate you. You, the members of our profession who belong to ACA, are the most highly conscious members of our profession. You are the ones who have chosen to belong to your professional association. You are the ones who pay the bills for all the others who are feeding off of the work that we do to maintain and advance our profession's role and status in society. You are the ones who know that, if ACA did not exist, you might have a tough time practicing your chosen profession. And if you could not do the job you love and have a passion for, you would be unhappy. See?

Now, all of us who practice this profession every day love our work. (Would you do something every day that you just did not like? If you responded "yes," I would suggest seeing a career counselor, and I know several good ones.)

We have a powerful message to bring to the world. And ACA's goal is to ensure the survival and growth of the counseling profession in the USA and around the world. But in order to do that, you've got to exist and, even better yet, thrive. The way that ACA continues to exist is through membership, that is, paying your dues. The more members, the better. Not just in terms of the economic health of the Association, but also in terms of political clout. The more of us there are, the more they listen to us on Capitol Hill and in every state capitol around the country (and even in the United Nations).

One of the truisms that I have learned in my many years in various organizations is that the way you get and keep members is by touching their professional lives, by providing relevant services. Such services must support professional issues such as getting and keep licensing, mandating and increasing funding for counselors in particular work settings such as the schools, economic parity with other mental health service providers, and many others. But it's always the economy. When you provide a service that is both relevant to their profession and touches them economically, you've got a winner!

And professional counseling didn't just happen. It was born because people like Donald Super and many others knew what had to be done to be certain that our profession could exist and provide help to all of those who are in emotional pain every day. And they knew that it takes an organized group of people to make a profession. They knew that it takes protracted, focused effort from a large number of people to make this all happen. And that it takes much hard work and dedication to make this all happen, year after year. You've got to have competencies, standards, ethics, certification, licensing, and all that it takes to make a profession happen.

I am an old "organization" warrior. I belong to a lot of organizations because I want to change the world and I (probably) can't do it alone. A wise person I once met in one of my other organizations told me that "money is congealed consciousness." I was profoundly moved by that statement. We spend our money in ways that reflect our values, what is important to us. So, when we choose not to belong to ACA or a Division or a Branch, we are saying that membership is not valued by us and, if that entity ceased to exist, it would be okay with us. Maybe we are not saying that consciously and maybe not with malicious intent, but that is the direct result of such actions on our part.

So, as a professional counselor, a member of a great profession that helps the world every day, one person and group at a time, I want to ask you to show your professionalism and support your profession. So here, for your consideration, is my recommended list of "To Do's for Today" for all of us. Ready? You might want to tear this out and put it on your refrigerator at home to refer to on an as-needed basis.

1. Join and actively participate in ACA
2. Join and actively participate in at least one Division (e.g., Counseling Association for Humanistic Education and Development)

3. Join and actively participate in your Branch (e.g., Rhode Island Counseling Association)
4. Register for and attend the ACA convention
5. Register for and attend at least one Division conference
6. Register for and attend your Branch convention

Now, I can already see you taking out your calculator and trying to figure out how much this is going to cost you. Let me try to help put this into perspective. I have a handy-dandy rule of thumb that I use to determine what I expect to spend for my professional development, to keep up-to-date as a professional. I call it my "10% rule." (I'm pretty sure it comes from my old Baptist days when we were expected to tithe 10% to our church.) Anyway, I budget a minimum of 10% of my annual salary for my professional development. If I make a salary of $25,000 per year, I expect to annually spend $2,500 on professional association dues and attending conferences and workshops. (I actually spend more than 10%, but that's just me.) Do you think that 10% is too much to invest back into your profession to ensure that the work that we do will be perpetuated? I also know that 10% can be a lot when you don't have much. I just want you to have a goal, a benchmark, and try.

But I have an even better question. What is it going to cost you (and our society) if your professional association ceases to exist? Okay, I'm being dramatic, but I want you to own and feel your professional responsibility in dramatic ways.

So, now that I have done my best to motivate you, I hope to see you in Kansas City for the upcoming ACA Convention. I also want you to promise to bring another professional counselor who hasn't been to our Convention before and maybe isn't even a current member. You'll both have a great time along with 3,000 of your closest friends. Remember: it's your professional responsibility, it's fun, you'll learn something, and it's a good thing. I'm also trying to get Mom to come there so you all can meet her.

Note: This chapter was originally published as the "ACA President's Column" in the February 2004 issue of *Counseling Today*.

Chapter 5

Counseling: The Best Kept Little Secret in the World

Shhhh. Don't tell anyone. It's a secret. Well, it's okay to tell your spouse or partner. Maybe a few close friends, but certainly not large, powerful people or groups like your school board, or teachers, or your city council, or the president of the company you work for, or, heaven forbid, the local newspaper, radio, or TV station.

The best kept little secret in the world is our profession—professional counseling.

Now, I can hear you all already vehemently declaring, "Not me. I don't keep our profession a secret. It's them (pointing your finger away from yourself)." Okay, maybe you are not the problem and the real problem is all our colleagues who are hiding this from the world, but I have been studying this issue and observing us over the past 30 years of my career and I have concluded that, while you (or they) are not doing this intentionally or consciously, you are contributing. I also know that this conclusion is based on mere observational data not collected in any intentional way, and so I am willing to allow that I may be wrong. But I don't think so. (Please send alternate data to pope@umsl.edu.)

Futher, I have this feeling (feelings are data, by the way, especially for those of us who can consistently and consciously access them) that you *wish* that the opposite were true—that everyone did know about what good professional counseling can do to help change a person's life, and, by extension, even the world.

I also know that all ACA members (well, at least a whole bunch) have a passion for our work. We love counseling and believe in the good we do in the world or else we just wouldn't do it. We want to help others. We see the power of counseling to create positive change in people's lives. And, we are in our profession for the long run. Good! Then, you are the ones that I want to talk to here.

So why doesn't everyone in the whole world know about who we are and what we do? (Another question that leaves me sleepless at night. Hey, as ACA President, it's my job.)

I have developed several hypotheses, presented here for you to ponder when you are sleepless as well.

Hypothesis #1: It's simply a skill problem. You are just not sure how to let everyone know. You're a counselor, not a trained public relations director. If you had wanted to go into business and marketing, you'd have an MBA now (and be making a lot more money). Right?

Hypothesis #2: It's simply an energy problem. Sometimes you just get tired of educating the whole world about who we are and what we do. This is for those who do have those specialized skills, but are just tired of marketing our profession every day. With everyone you meet, you have to begin all over again and tell them what counseling is about and how it changed your (or another person's) life. Blah, blah, blah. You are just tired of it—and a bit cynical because nobody seems to just get it without you having to teach, teach, teach all the time.

Hypothesis #3: It's simply a personality problem. Sort of an occupational hazard. According to our best and most current research, we who are most attracted to our profession tend to have RIASEC codes (come on, you remember these from your career counseling or assessment courses) that look like this—SAE. Our career interest patterns are built on a primary foundation of "S" or "Social." People like this want to help PEOPLE, not build a house (things or Realistic), or do bookkeeping (data or Conventional). Now, I know that this will come as no surprise to you, but most of you don't have a lot of the old Enterprising interest. Business people, especially managers, small business owners, or salespeople who are effective and successful have a lot of "E" or "Enterprising," including marketing and public relations types. Now, don't get me wrong. Some of us do, and a whole bunch of those types of professional counselors are either career counselors or in some type of full-time independent practice. It's just that it is not a predominate interest within most of us.

Hypothesis #4: It's simply a misunderstanding. There is an unwritten "code of silence" out there. It probably comes about through our ethics training around confidentiality. We have somehow interpreted our ethical code as including keeping the name and purpose of our profession confidential. (By the way, I have consulted our Standing Committee on Ethics and Task Force on the Ethics Code Revision and both have verified that this interpretation is incorrect.) This hypothesis is my favorite one, by the way.

Hypothesis #5: It's simply a "should" problem. It should just be obvious to others what an important role counseling plays in our society and in our lives. It probably "should" be, but I fear that it isn't.

Hypothesis #6: It's simply a value problem. One of the values that many counselors have and live by is humility. When we do something good, we say "no big deal" because we are a humble lot. We think this is a positive attribute and value that we seek to cultivate. In most of the work that we do in our profession, this is not a problem; however, it is here.

Hypothesis #7: It's simply a "not my responsibility" issue. Wrong. We can't simply think that someone else will do it. It doesn't work that way. When you receive your graduate degree in our profession, you take on certain professional responsibilities. This is simply one of them. It is your responsibility as a professional counselor to carry this message to others, everyday of your life, as long as you live, work, or breathe. (Note the use of the word "or.") It is our responsibility not just to us, or to our family and friends, but also to our community and to the society in which we live. My mother (Ethyle) told me that we have a responsibility to leave the world a better place than when we entered it. I listen to my mother as she is rarely wrong (just like your mother, I'm sure).

Bottomline is that I am not asking you to go against your personality type and career interests, or to take up marketing as a new career path, but I do want you to develop some new important competencies and to do just a little more.

All I am asking is that you begin to nurture some new skills.

I would like you to make one little promise to me. During the next month, you will tell one other person about the importance of counseling. This first month I want you to start with someone you know personally. Next month your assignment is a person who you don't know. Next month tell your local school principal. Next month tell a local school board member. Next month, your city council. Next month, your employer or, if you are in private practice, tell a local business that does not offer employee assistance counseling as a benefit to its workers. And then tell your state and national legislators, frequently and regularly.

All I am asking for here is that you become a marketer of professional counseling to all of our external constituencies, broadly defined as government leaders in each branch (executive, legislative, and even judicial) at every level (local, state, national, and international), business and industry, other professional associations, schools, nongovernmental organizations, and consumers.

Also, the next time you do something good (even if you are not in independent practice or a career counselor), I want you to prepare a "media release" (what we used to call a "press release"). But it will go to more than a newspaper (printed on a "press," get it). I want you to also send it to your local radio station and television station (hence "media"). Begin by getting the email address of your local media. Then get a JPG image of yourself and attach it electronically to your media release and e-mail all this to your local media—newspapers, radio, and television stations. This may sound like a lot to do, but the potential payoff for you and for all of us is huge.

My colleagues, what we have is just too important to keep secret. It is our professional responsibility to let the rest of the world know how critical professional counseling is to individuals, to our communities, and to our world. We have to market our profession, frequently and regularly, and not hide our profession under a basket (or any other culturally appropriate symbol). Each of us individually and collectively must take responsibility for marketing our profession to the world. It is time to come out to the rest of the world and proclaim the tremendous worth of our profession joyously and energetically.

I will be checking with each of you later on your progress. (Hope you are enjoying this.) By the way, Mom says "hi!"

———————

Note: This chapter was originally published as the "ACA President's Column" in the October 2003 issue of *Counseling Today*.

Chapter 6

We Should All Be
As Good As Mary Arnold

This is not going to be a happy column. My dear friend, fellow traveler, and colleague, Mary Arnold passed away in the beginning of October. Mary was a professor (one who professes) at Governors State University in Chicago along with Judy Lewis, Julia Tang, Jon Carlson, Hugh Crethar, Cyrus Ellis, and several other truly outstanding professors. She was a tireless fighter for the little guy, for those abused by the system.

I fell in love with her from the moment I met her and became a card-carrying member of the Mary Arnold Fan Club. At that time, she was a faculty member at Kent State University, and Mary and I were both attending the Association for Counselor Education and Supervision (ACES) national conference in San Antonio. One of the keynote events during that conference was a multicultural counseling experts panel, moderated by Courtland Lee. Clemmont Vontress, one of the panelists, was considered by many to be one of the founders of multicultural counseling and a major contributor to our profession. During his presentation, he made his case for a definition of multiculturalism that included only racial and ethnic minorities and excluded sexual minorities and any other diversity issue. According to Dr. Vontress, there was no room at the multicultural counseling table for a gay and lesbian "culture." During the Q&A session that followed, the first seven questioners all directed their comments to Dr. Vontress, disagreeing with his exclusive definition. I was the first questioner and Mary Arnold was second. Here she was, this strong, steely-eyed African American woman taking on the great Clemmont Vontress, one of the African American icons of our profession, and taking him to task for the narrowness of his views on culture. She was respectful but nonetheless a fighter for what she thought was right, and she became my hero instantly.

Later, Mary and I were both part of the founding of Counselors for Social Justice (CSJ), and at the organizing meeting at ACA headquarters we all stood around the big conference room table holding hands and sharing our feelings and vision for the counseling profession. A profession that had its roots in the late

1800s and early 1900s and in the progressive social reform movements of that time focused on child labor and the exploitation of children in the industrial factories. We all wanted to help recover those roots for our entire profession. When CSJ became a full Division, Mary Arnold was the first CSJ representative to the ACA Governing Council. Her voice was strong, never failing to ask us to look deeper at an issue and focus on what was really important.

Then, I was fortunate enough to talk Mary into coming to St. Louis to keynote a professional development conference for the school counselors in the St. Louis Public Schools. It is a conference that we at the University of Missouri–St. Louis conduct every year. She was magnificent as she addressed their questions and concerns. She made each of them feel that they were tremendously important in the care and psychological feeding of our inner-city children. She told them that they made a difference every day in the lives of these children. And they believed her because she spoke from her heart. She was wise, very wise, and she cared so very deeply. You could always see that in her face, the way she carried herself, in every behavior. She carried the world in her heart and shared it with us all.

When I got the news of Mary's passing, it was Sunday morning and I was in Washington, DC. It was the last day of our traditional fall Governing Council meeting—the final day of four days of intensive presentation and discussion highly charged with critical issues for our profession. I was presiding, we had a too-full agenda, and I am a task-oriented person. Part of me wished that I had heard about Mary after the meeting, but once you heard that she had passed, there was no turning back. I was hit hard by this news. Many of us at the Governing Council were hit hard, and as I told those present of Mary's passing, I heard audible gasps followed quickly by sobs from your Governors. With tears in our eyes, we took time to process this loss and, for those who could, talk about our memories of Mary. We then stood around the big circle, holding hands for a moment of solemn tribute to one of our fallen comrades.

Mary, who had ended her term as the CSJ representative to the Governing Council in June, was not physically at this meeting, but her presence was felt as always. Mary always had a flare for the dramatic and I'm pretty sure she was watching as we stood, held hands, and cried during this Governing Council meeting.

See, Mary Arnold had a professional identity that was big enough for the whole world. She epitomized what I think is the best in our profession—caring about others and always reminding both us and the world to remember our humanity. I have this distinct impression that Professor Frank Parsons (professional counseling's founder) would have been proud of her and what we have become and he would also be grieving over our loss. I am certain that he would have felt that we should all be as good as Mary Arnold. Me too.

And I already miss her greatly.

Note: This chapter was originally published as the "ACA President's Column" in the November 2003 issue of Counseling Today.

Part III

Contextual and Cultural
Development

Chapter 7

First We Are Sane, Now We Are Legal

June 26, 2003. Does that date mean anything to you? How about December 15, 1973? The Ides of December? Eight days after the Japanese bombing of Pearl Harbor (over 30 years earlier)? Uncle Ned's birthday? Yes, yes, and hardly.

These two dates—almost 30 years apart—are two of the most historic dates ever regarding the civil rights of gays and lesbians in the USA.

On December 15, 1973, the American Psychiatric Association's Board of Trustees overwhelmingly voted to remove "homosexuality" from its list of mental disorders (the *Diagnostic and Statistical Manual of Mental Disorders; DSM-2*). They found that "[h]omosexuality per se implies no impairment in judgment, stability, reliability, or general social and vocational capabilities." (Dr. Evelyn Hooker reported those data in the 1960s as part of her ground-breaking study of gay men. Dr. Alfred Kinsey and his colleagues at Indiana University found similar results.) By this vote, lesbians and gays, therefore, became "sane" overnight. (Yes, I know that I am stretching the definition of the term, but just bear with me for now.) (By the way, opponents of the decision attempted to overturn it with a referendum of the ApA membership in early 1974. The Board's decision to delete homosexuality from the diagnostic manual was supported by 58% of their membership. The opponents of progress don't ever go down easily.)

Then, on June 26, 2003, in the most significant governmental ruling ever for lesbian and gay Americans' civil rights, the U.S. Supreme Court struck down Texas's sodomy law, which had criminalized oral and anal sex by consenting gay couples and was used widely to justify discrimination against lesbians and gay men in Lawrence and Garner v. Texas. This effectively overturned all the remaining 13 state sodomy laws in the USA. Similar to Plessy v. Ferguson; Brown v. The Board of Education of Topeka, Kansas; and Roe v. Wade, Lawrence and Garner v. Texas is a landmark judicial decision. Gay men and lesbians became legal throughout the entire USA overnight.

What Brown v. The Board of Education of Topeka, Kansas did in 1964 for the struggle for the civil rights of African Americans, Lawrence and Garner

v. Texas has now done for lesbian, gay, and bisexual Americans. Even the justices on the Supreme Court who dissented from the majority opinion (Rehnquist, Scalia, and Thomas), went out of their way to state that they were not in favor of this law. Justice Clarence Thomas, one of the Court's most conservative members, even went so far as to note that "punishing someone for expressing his sexual preference through noncommercial consensual conduct with another adult does not appear to be a worthy way to expend valuable law enforcement resources" and he called it "a silly law," quoting Justice Potter Stewart's dissent in Griswold v. Connecticut.

By now, most of you have heard all of the details, but for those of you who have been vacationing, let me summarize briefly. In the middle of the night, John Geddes Lawrence and Tyron Garner were dragged out of Mr. Lawrence's apartment, arrested, and forced to spend the night in jail, after officers responding to a false report found the men engaged in private, consensual sex. The two men were frightened, shocked, and humiliated. Once convicted, they were forced to pay fines and were then considered sex offenders in several states prior to this ruling.

By a vote of 6–3 and as the final act of the United States Supreme Court for its current term, the Supreme Court made a strong stand for the rights of lesbian and gay Americans. In 1960, every state in the USA had a sodomy law on the books; in 1986, half the states did. As of June 25, 2003, only 13 states remained "hold-outs." Of the 13 states with sodomy laws, four—Texas, Kansas, Oklahoma, and Missouri—prohibit oral and anal sex between same-sex couples. The other nine ban consensual sodomy for everyone: Alabama, Florida, Idaho, Louisiana, Mississippi, North Carolina, South Carolina, Utah, and Virginia.

Why is this of importance or of interest to professional counselors? Because such laws affect the lives of our clients, students, family, friends, and colleagues. How does such an antiquated and rarely used law affect these lives? Such laws are widely used to justify discrimination against gay people in everyday life. Such laws stigmatize lesbians and gay men in many ways. In addition to branding lesbians and gay men as criminals, these laws are used to deny employment, to deny child custody and visitation rights, and as a rationale against enacting civil rights laws that bar discrimination based on sexual orientation. (An online video is available which explains how sodomy laws have been used against lesbians and gay men in everyday life (at http://www.lambdalegal.org/cgi-bin/iowa/documents/record?record=1272).

Here are just a few examples of the thousands available:

- A Virginia State Legislator who oversees a committee responsible for reappointing judges across the state said he opposes reappointing a local judge to a second term if she is a lesbian and is violating the state's sodomy law.
- In Texas, a lesbian foster mother lost her foster child when a state social worker invoked the "emergency authority" the state gives of-

ficials to remove children when there is ongoing "criminal activity" in the foster home. The foster mother's only "criminal activity" was being a lesbian in a state with a sodomy law.

- The Board of Curators of the University of Missouri system cited the fact that such a sodomy law exists in Missouri as an argument to not prohibit discrimination based on sexual orientation and to not allow domestic partner benefits for students, faculty, or staff.
- It is both sad and ironic that on December 14, 1973, gay and lesbian Americans were insane. And then on December 15, 1973, a mere 24 hours later, we were sane. It almost seems like magic. (Insert wry smile about here.)
- Similarly, in the 13 states that still had sodomy laws on June 25, 2003, we were illegal. And then on June 26, 2003, a mere 24 hours later, we became immediately legal.

Some day in the future, I'd even be willing to bet that there will be a vote by the delegates of the Southern Baptist Convention or an encyclical from the Pope (not me, by the way) of the Roman Catholic Church or an essay from the Hassidic Rabbi Yitzchak Ginsburgh that says that gays and lesbians are also now moral. Poof. Overnight. What a glorious day that will be for all of us who are lesbian or gay and who have been regularly disparaged in certain quarters as the pinnacle of all sin. (I do wonder how two men or two women loving one another and making a home and family together suddenly got to be the preeminent sin in the world. But, I'm a traditional Cherokee— we didn't even know there was such a sin hierarchy until the missionaries came.)

Gay men and lesbian women have gone from being sane to being legal in (only) 30 years. Now that we are both sane and legal, can moral be far behind?

Note: This chapter was originally published as the "ACA President's Column" in the August 2003 issue of *Counseling Today*. It has been revised for inclusion here.

Chapter 8

Multiculturalism Belongs to All of Us

Now that I have your attention, I may be beating a dead horse, but I have the stick and it's my turn. (Colorful image, eh? Must be my Midwestern agrarian upbringing or my Cherokee storytelling training.) I want to talk with you today about the multicultural movement within our profession.

Way back in 1991, Paul Pedersen was the editor for a special issue of our flagship journal, the *Journal of Counseling & Development*. He wrote that multicultural counseling was the fourth force in the building of our counseling movement. (I know that you are aware of what the other three were, but for those who were dozing during that multicultural counseling lecture— the other forces have been psychodynamic, behavioral, and humanist.) This special issue was an important broadside in the intellectual war for the soul of our profession. It was the beginning of a movement that has changed the face of our profession, literally and figuratively. It is a movement that has broadened our analyses, diagnoses, and interventions to include the macro level of group, community, and society. In some ways, this has been a re-integration of our social work roots that we had previously discarded for our more individual psychology clinical orientation.

Now, I know that there are some of you out there who are tired of culture and discussions about culture. You are the more conservative elements of us, and you have just had it with multicultural this and multicultural that. All you hear is multicultural, multicultural, multicultural. And, further, you have just had it with people who are going to tell you about the "truth" one more time. You tend to be part of the dominant culture of your society (however that is defined) and think that the problem lies within people rather than the external environment. You think that the multicultural people are whiners and one-note wonders who are always looking for institutional scapegoats and who never allow their clients any individual responsibility. Further, you can't seem to find a place for yourself at the multicultural table and wonder what all the fuss is about. You tend to be more psychodynamic in your professional orientation and want to have more focus on intrapsychic phenomena.

Then there is another group of you who can't get enough of all of this talk about the culture, context, environment, or milieu in which our clients operate. You are part of the more progressive or liberal elements of us. You are the true believers. You are generally part of some cultural community that is a target of the dominant culture. You live and work with oppression every day. You see the world in these types of ways—who is the oppressor (dominant culture) and who is the oppressed (target culture). Your theoretical orientation is generally multicultural counseling and therapy or some other cognitive/behavioral approach.

(Please forgive my broadbrush approach here, but I'm trying to make a point.)

And both groups are afraid. And if you need to be afraid, I want you to acknowledge it, be aware of it, feel it, and let it pass through you (Gestalt technique). (Now, let me see if I can make everyone mad.)

The first group is afraid that our profession is being taken over by leftwing radical revolutionists who have a social justice policy agenda that will advance their social views while obliterating our most important professional issues, like licensing, standards, Medicare reimbursement, and the overall recognition and acceptance of our profession within our society (what I call "guild" issues).

The second group is afraid that our profession is filled with a bunch of do-gooder liberals who want to water down the race issue in our profession and society by bringing in all these other "–isms" and that they will be left out when we get to the promised land, of sweetness and light and milk and honey, etc.

Fortunately or unfortunately, like with most stereotypes, there is a grain of truth in each point of view.

And now you are saying, "good analysis" or alternatively "he's pathetic" (especially if you disagree with me).

Anyway, so what?

I and most of my predecessors in the ACA Presidency find ourselves caught somewhere in the middle, but with definite leanings. My two rules to live by as ACA President are: (1) always take care of the guild issues first, then the social justice issues; and (2) the more we understand that we all are part of multiple cultures and begin to analyze the world in that manner, the more we understand the race issue.

I'm not going to spend a lot of time with the first rule, because it is quite self-explanatory. The reason I am in the leadership of the American Counseling Association is because I believe passionately in the work that we do. Passionately. My primary role now and in the future is to make certain—in all that I do and with my entire being—that our profession continues and prospers. And I can do that easily because I believe passionately (third time in one paragraph) in the work that we do, about the good that we do in our world everyday. We help ease the pain and suffering of all humanity. It's a simple rule, but powerful in its simplicity.

Rule two is more complex, but very important to understand. I have this feeling that, in our teaching and practice of multicultural counseling, some of us focus on a narrower, exclusive definition of culture. We talk about racial and ethnic issues, but rarely do we talk about the cultures of sexual orientation, age, gender, geographic location (urban, suburban, rural), physical ability (physically able or challenged), religion and spirituality, or social economy (socio-economic status).

There is another group of us out there who use a broader, more inclusive and universal definition of culture in our teachings about multicultural counseling. We want to help our students see culture as something that everyone has. We want to help our students "get it" and understand that they too are a part of a culture, really many cultures. Then it becomes exciting to share your cultures with others and to explore other cultures. It opens more of us up to discussions about culture and to examining our own issues, and few then feel "left out."

Some multiculturalists have differentiated between a culture and a "diversity issue." (Sometimes I feel that it's like a competition to see who's more oppressed or who ought to be allowed into the oppression "club," where "culture" is better and "diversity issue" is somehow second class.) In my worldview, all this does is limit the potential impact on society of multiculturalism and its ideas. If the ideas of the multicultural movement win, we (our profession, our clients, our society, our world) all win whether we are African American, gay, disabled, or live in a rural area . . . or even a White European urban male.

That said, we must always remember that the race issue in the US is the central issue for our society (remember, we fought a war over this). But, some see this more inclusive definition of culture as a watering down of the race issue and that we must confront our students' and colleagues' racism actively and aggressively wherever we find it. And I agree, we must. Just as we must identify and confront our own issues whatever they may be.

See, denial of or actively refusing to confront any such personal issue is a recipe for disaster as a professional counselor and in our profession.

I am willing to make this very bold statement: You cannot be a excellent or even good professional counselor without addressing your own issues of prejudice—racism, sexism, ageism, heterosexism, ableism, geographicism, and others. Your awareness of your own capacity to prejudge is critical to your ability to function effectively as a professional counselor.

The first statement that I make in the multicultural classes I teach is that "we all have racial prejudices." I sometimes state it as "we are all racist," until later when we talk about racism (or any –ism) and how it is also about power and who has (or doesn't have) it. You simply cannot grow up in a racist, sexist, ageist, heterosexist, ableist (and others) society without having aspects of this yourself. And . . . you can't get better until you openly acknowledge this fact of our common humanity.

For me, one of my goals as a practicing professional counselor is to help individuals take their unconscious thoughts and feelings to the conscious level. "Oh, I'm not prejudiced," is one of my favorite statements in a session or a class, because my experience tells me that we are all prejudiced, but only when we are aware of our prejudices do we have any real control over them. Only then can we actively confront our own issues. (I know it's awfully psychodynamic, but it makes sense to me. I hope I'm not one of those "eclectic" practitioners. Yecch.)

I know that this may be a radical idea, but counseling absolutely means change. (Hey, the change may be only accepting yourself, but many times that's the biggest change of all.) The question for me as a professional counselor is how to be the most effective agent for change. This requires constantly examining yourself—honestly and sometimes painfully—but nevertheless doing it. It's a funny thing, but the emotional, physical, and economic comfort that many of us seek in our lives is sometimes that which keeps us from growing. At the other end of that continuum, too much pain produces the same effect. But sometimes we need a little discomfort to move on. I hope I provide a "little discomfort" in your professional life.

Okay, I'm done.

Note: This chapter was originally published as the "ACA President's Column" in the April 2004 issue of *Counseling Today*.

Chapter 9

When You Meet Strangers
on the Road, Embrace Them

was in a little town a while ago called Dawn, Texas. I was driving through just as the sun was rising (the serendipity of this was not lost on me). So, I stopped at a little gas station there to get fuel and check my water and found myself engaged in a discussion with Gus, who owned the station. I'm not really sure how it all started, but Gus and I were chit-chatting about the beautiful sunrise and he began to talk about how "them Mexicans" were moving in. Now, Gus was definitely a "good ol' boy" who talked with a Texas twang and had a neck that looked like a beet. And I immediately thought I knew where he was going, but good old Gus surprised me, quite pleasantly.

See, Gus told me that he was married to a wonderful woman who was originally from Mexico. He told me how she had come to the United States from her native Mexico in the back of a hot, enclosed truck along with 30 others. How she had almost died in that truck. And how he had come to meet her and fall in love with her and how they now had four of the most beautiful children in the world. His wife was a citizen now, because the laws allowed him to marry whomever he wanted and to allow her to stay in the US since they were married. He pulled out his wallet to show me pictures of his wife, Carmelinda, and their children, and he then told me of the difficulties that his multi-ethnic children were having at the local school and some of the difficulties that he and his wife had from some of his old friends who were not supportive of his marriage to Carmelinda. He had different friends now. But his children were being called all sorts of names at their school and no one was doing anything about it. And he was angry. This kind of stuff wasn't supposed to be happening to him, just because he married someone who wasn't like them (his old friends). He told me that he had been that way once, but he "saw the light" because of his wonderful wife and his beautiful children. And he said, "I was a real redneck once, but no more."

Then he went on to say that he really had begun to think about a whole lot of similar issues too. Like the civil rights of a whole lot of different people from the Civil War to Japanese internment camps and even gay marriage.

And he wanted to talk about gay marriage because he had heard about that most recently. The way he figured it, "If two people love each other, the damn government ought to at least just stay out of their way." He thought that amending the US Constitution to prohibit gay marriage was just "silly" and it made him mad. "We tried another type of prohibition once and that didn't work out too well." He said it was just like his marriage to Carmelinda, "No government ought to be telling me who I can marry and who I can't, who I can love and who I can't. That's just not right."

I asked him about the religious aspect of marriage. He said, "As long as it's the government giving those licenses, them gay people shouldn't be told no. They're Americans too. A priest or preacher should have the right to say who they'll marry and who they won't, and if a church says they won't marry some people because they aren't fit for some reason or other, that's their right too, but not a government. . . . That there President said we went to Iraq to fight for freedom, but who's freedom are we fightin' for? Freedom begins at home."

About that time, two of Gus and Carmelinda's children came into the station. They were beautiful children, as Gus had warranted, and they were on their way to school.

I gave them my business card and I told them to have their school counselor call me. Maybe a little talk would be a good place to start. (It's what ACA presidents do.)

I paid for my gas and left Dawn, TX, but I got a feeling that Gus and Dawn, TX will be part of my life from now on.

By the way, March is National No Name-Calling Month. Thought you'd like to know. Maybe a little talk would be a good place to start.

Note: This chapter was origianlly written as a President's Column in *Counseling Today,* but got bumped by other timely events.

Part IV

Organizational Development

Chapter 10

The History of Our World: Part One (or Professions Don't Just Happen Overnight)

History is (many times) boring. Important, but . . . boring. I want to apologize upfront for this, but professions don't just happen overnight. We come from something and become something else. And as someone once said, "Those who do not understand history are doomed to repeat the same mistakes."

One reason that I talk about the history of professional counseling is because I am a trained political scientist and historian as well as professional counselor. So, it's all of great interest to me (sorry). But, I am also talking about ACA and where we came from because I want you to understand and appreciate our/your history and, therefore, strengthen your professional identity. We have a magnificent history.

A few introductory remarks to guide your reading.

One, look for the word "human" as you read this. You learn a lot about a profession by the words we use. We use "human" a lot, as in "human being" and "humanity." Good strong words to understand, especially if you are a professional counselor or want to be one.

Two, I'm going to ask you to stay with me. You know, in the text. Because I know that this can be deadly boring. Try to get through it without dozing. (Good reading at night before you go to bed.)

Three, here are some questions to guide your reading. (Just as in all of your life, this is the quiz they promised you. The good news is that I'm giving you the questions first.)

1. Who is considered the founder of counseling?
2. What was the original name of ACA?
3. Who was the second president of ACA?
4. What were the names of the founding Divisions of ACA?
5. What does CACREP stand for and when was it founded?
6. What state had the first professional counseling licensure law?
7. Which Branch was chartered first?

(Yeah, I feel your pain, sorry. Please stay with me.)

Time for a story: Once upon a time, a long time ago, far away from Alabama (please feel free to insert any appropriate location in the place of Alabama—I just happened to be there for this talk), a profession was born. In 1952 in Chicago, a group of vocational guidance counselors and counseling psychologists and college counselors and deans of students and university professors met. They decided that there was more strength in larger numbers of us working together than in simply working apart. (Pay attention. These are the answers to questions 2 and 4 on the quiz. I'm trying to make it easy for you.) The four groups that came together to form the nucleus of this new Association—then called the American Personnel and Guidance Association (APGA), later to be called the American Counseling Association (ACA)—were the National Vocational Guidance Association (NVGA) (later to be called the National Career Development Association; NCDA), the American College Personnel Association (ACPA), the Student Personnel Association for Teacher Education (SPATE) (now known as the Counseling Association for Humanistic Education and Development; C-AHEAD), and the National Association of Guidance and Counselor Trainers (NAGCT) (now know as the Association for Counselor Education and Supervision; ACES) (McDaniels, 1964).

The biggest group and the one with the most money was NVGA. They had a journal (*Occupations: The Vocational Guidance Journal*—snappy name, eh?). They had an Executive Director and they had a headquarters building and they had Mary Janicke (pronounced 'Jan ick e' (long e)). They gave all of this to APGA (now ACA). Nice human beings, eh? Well, they didn't give Mary Janicke to APGA, but Mary came along with the package and currently works as the Secretary to the ACA President. She is a gem!

1952 v. 2002

In 1952, when the ACA was born, the world was a very different place. The chart that follows shows what the United States looked like at that time.

By the way, the 1950 census data also included what we would now think of as rather esoteric data such as the number of households that had a flush toilet inside their home for their exclusive use (that means "not shared with another home") along with a listing of the type of refrigeration equipment used in homes, which included mechanical (80%), ice (10.7%), and none (8.7%) (My Mom still calls it the "ice box."). Almost 90% of the households reported having no television while 69.1% of farm households did not have either a bathtub or shower (when I told this to my Mom (she's kind of a character) she said she hoped that those 69% weren't pig farmers—that's my Mom). Only 2.2% of individuals who rented homes paid $100 or more, and the average monthly rent was $39.

I won't provide you with the 2002 flush toilet statistics (although I do have them available for those of you who are interested, please email me at pope@umsl.edu), but I think you get the picture.

	1952	2002
Population	151 million	281 million
Resides in	67% urban	75% urban
At least an undergraduate degree	6.2%	13.6%
People not born in the US	Italy (14%)	Mexico (21%)
	Asia (1.8%)	Asia (17%)
	Mexico (4.4%)	
African Americans	15 million (10%)[a]	34 million (12%)[b]
"Other races"	713,000 (0.5%)	14.9% (total)
"Hispanic"		10.7%
"Asian and Pacific Islander"		3.5%
"American Indian and Eskimo"		0.7%
California population	10 million	34 million
Labor force in agriculture	11%	2.4%
Top 10 cities by population	New York	New York
	Chicago	Los Angeles
	Philadelphia	Chicago
	Los Angeles	Houston
	Detroit	Philadelphia
	Baltimore	San Diego
	Cleveland	Phoenix
	St. Louis	San Antonio
	Washington, DC	Dallas
	Boston	Detroit

Note. From U. S. Census Bureau, 2000.
[a]1952 called "Negro." [b]2002 called "non-Hispanic Black."

Welcome to more than 50 years of changes. And welcome to more than 50 years as a profession.

Factors Leading to the Growth of Counseling

Obviously, with all of those demographic changes, there has also been a change in the kind of people that we serve as well. And, because of these changes, our profession has also had to change.

We are a profession, in fact, that was born and has historically seen our largest growth as a direct result of the problems that human beings have when societies change. When society is in transition from one socio-economic period to another, this creates individual stress and personal trauma. Back in the early 1900s, if you made leather harnesses for horses that pulled plows, you might have to be retrained to make machine parts for the tractors that replaced those animals. But such changes are not made easily in a society. (You knew that.) And they are made with great individual and familial turmoil. *Counselors help ease that pain of transition.*

ACA was founded in 1952, but the history of professional counseling goes back much further than the founding of ACA. At the beginning of counseling (And by the way, some of you who are reading this were there. I'm not naming names, but you know who you are.) in the late 1800s, there was a maverick in the social work movement. (Pay attention: this is the answer to question 1 on your quiz.) His name was Frank Parsons. Now, Professor Parsons began his career working as a social worker heavily influenced by Jane Addams's work at Hull House in Chicago. Professor Parsons established the Vocation Bureau at the Civic Service House in Boston in 1908. He was a maverick because no one in social work was doing this. This "settlement house" (think of it as a "resettlement" house that helped people get resettled after they had just moved to the city from somewhere else—rural America, Eastern Europe, or wherever) program was for young people who were already employed or currently unemployed and had moved to Boston to get good-paying jobs in this new industrial economy. This was the first institutionalization of career counseling and, really, any kind of counseling in the US. (I probably should have put that on the quiz.)

And the foundation for Parsons's career counseling was assessment. It was built on matching the characteristics of a person with those of an occupation, or what we now call in our profession a Trait–Factor or Person–Environment Fit strategy.

As a short aside that I think that you all may appreciate (or not), Professor Parsons also dabbled in the use of phrenology as a scientific method of determining a person's personality and career interests—you all know what phrenology is, I'm sure, but for those of you who are untrained in the esoterica of assessment and want to add a new (or old) tool to your intervention toolbox, phrenology is a technique in which the counselor feels the head of a person with their hands, noticing where there are bumps, indentations, holes, etc., which are then interpreted as being associated with certain individual characteristics. Hey, it's a theory. I am, unfortunately, unfamiliar with the many volumes of phrenology research published since then (this is supposed to be funny, and I sincerely hope that you are at least enjoying a wry smile), but let us say that it is a technique rarely used these days (in professional counseling anyway).

What is important for you to know is that we are a profession born from *change*. A profession that has grown both numerically and in importance as a direct result of social upheaval and change. From the beginning of our profession, each stage in our professional history was preceded by a major societal change. And each of these changes (like a world war or cultural or economic revolution) has had profound effects on the lives of human beings in our society. The role of professional counseling has always grown during such times, as a response to these immense social changes. (If you have gotten this far, stay with me. It gets even better.)

Foundations of Professional Counseling

There are six historic factors that have been identified as the foundation of professional counseling. Each of these six factors (career counseling, assessment, humanism, school guidance, medicine, and multiculturalism) has been important to the development of our professional identity (Pope, 2000).

I'm only going to discuss (briefly, very briefly—stay with me) three of these factors in particular as they relate especially to change and also to illustrate our core values as a profession.

The first factor that laid the foundation for our entire profession was career counseling. (I sincerely hope that I have not yet lost all of the people who want to be psychotherapists.) Career counseling was born in the USA in the early 1900s out of societal upheaval, transition, and change. This new profession was described by historians of that time as (and I want you to read these words carefully as they are critical to your understanding of our entire profession) a "progressive social reform movement aimed at eradicating poverty and substandard living conditions spawned by the rapid industrialization and consequent migration of people to major urban centers at the turn of the 20th century" (Whiteley, 1984, p. 2). (Again, that's really important. Not on the quiz, but important.)

Participants in those early days of the "career counseling movement" described it as a "calling." They had a *passion* to help the people who were being ground up in this social transition from an agricultural society to an industrial society. Here is what was happening. People were losing their jobs in the agricultural sector, while at the same time there were increasing demands for workers in heavy industry. There was a loss of "permanent" jobs on the family farm to emerging technologies such as tractors (hey, compared to horse-drawn plows, tractors are new technology). This led to an increasing movement to urban centers of the US, and then an increased need for services to meet this internal migration pattern. All of this in order to retool for this new industrial economy. Returning vets (that's veterans, not veterinarians) from World War I and those new workers who had taken the soldiers' places in the factories and were now being displaced by their return only heightened the need for career counseling.

Another factor in our developing professional identity was humanism and its political reflection, Progressivism. The earliest support for our profession came from the Progressive social reform movement (this was a real political party during that time, not just a generic word for liberal). "The linkage between this movement and vocational guidance was largely built on the issue of the growing exploitation and misuse of human beings" (Aubrey, 1977, p. 290). (See, there's that word "human" again.) Child labor laws provided the impetus for this collaboration as the crusade to prohibit the exploitation of children grew. Although some states had established minimum age laws in the latter half of the 19th century, the first decade of the 20th century continued to see over half of a million children from 10 to 13 years of age employed. And effective federal legislation did not come about until the passage of the 1938 Fair Labor Standards Act. Professor Frank Parsons was also a prominent leader in the struggle to eliminate child labor.

Finally, multiculturalism is the most recent factor in our developing professional identity. In the past 15 years there has been a strong trend in our profession to move away from medical models of counseling to more contextual models—to look at the context in which the individual operates as a critical issue in developing a way to approach the issues and problems that bring a client into our practice. In the past 50 years, with the growth of Latin American and Asian and Pacific Islander immigration to the US, we have seen a concomitant increase in the number and variety of ethnic and racial cultures in the US. We have seen a strengthening of the civil rights organizations of this country and a demand for the full rights of citizenship from African Americans, women, lesbians and gays, older people, those with disabilities, and more. This move to a greater emphasis in professional counseling on multicultural counseling skills is a direct result of the changing demographics of our society and the diverse needs of these cultural groups for help during their transitions.

Change and Diversity

As you can see, changes in our social fabric are forcing changes in the way we conduct our practice (as it should).

Change happens. So, what are we going to do?

Here in the United States, like many other countries, we are being confronted with the issues of change and diversity in our society: demographic, technological, educational, economic, familial, and career. The clients we will be seeing and the groups that we will be facilitating in the year 2013 will be different as a result of our changing demographics, and they will be confronting a very different situation in the world than ever before.

We must learn to value and appreciate these changes and our diversity rather than approach them with fear. Societies that appreciate, understand, and value their own diversity flourish. We have the opportunity now to change the way we approach the differences that are inherent in our world today.

See, I think that we have a message to bring to the world. I believe that one of the strengths of our profession lies in our message about valuing the broadly based multicultural "salad bowl" of our world. We cannot afford to waste one human being of any race, ethnic background, gender, sexual orientation, disability, or spiritual nature. (See, there's that word "human" again.)

(Go ahead, count the number of times that "human" is used in this paragraph alone.) I believe that our role in society is to keep **humanity** or **humaneness** (again, "human") in the world, to keep the focus on the person in our institutions. As many of you who work or have worked in large institutions such as businesses or schools know, people regularly get chewed up and spit out. Even though such institutions are operated by **human** beings, they can too easily lose their **humanity**. We all know about such institutions. Many of us have first-hand experience as victims of this. The role of counselors should be to aid both the victim as well as change the **inhuman** treatment of workers—to keep **humanity** in the institution. We must embrace the role of **human** beings in **inhumane** institutions. To be the spokesperson for the people who have no voice. (I like that paragraph a lot. "Human" (or a derivative) used eight times. Nice. And if you count the "persons" or "people" or "individual," then there's another four. Very nice.)

We, in the counseling profession, have an immense task. One that we as a profession are especially well suited for. We have a critical message to bring to our global society.

I also know that we professional counselors have a passion for our work. We love counseling and believe in the good we do in the world or else we just wouldn't do it. We want to help others. We see the power of counseling to create positive change in people's lives. And, we are in our profession for the long run.

Here's what I think we are all about. It comes from an article that was written in 1991 by one of my heroes, Ruth Fassinger. She spoke for so many of us who have chosen professional counseling over social work and other mental health professions, and she said it so eloquently:

> Inherent in our philosophy (as counselors) is an approach that frames problems in terms of normalcy and day-to-day problems in living, and eschews a singular focus on pathology and diagnosis. We emphasize positive mental health and focus on strengths and adaptive strategies in our clients. We see ourselves as educators and advocates for clients, and we emphasize the empowerment of individuals. We value preventive as well as ameliorative intervention efforts, and we work toward enhanced functioning of all people. Our scope of vision includes environmental as well as individual interventions, promotion of mental health at the level of groups and systems, the effective use of community resources, and political involvement where relevant. We see ourselves as versatile, able to function in a variety of settings and to work collegially with other diverse professionals. We emphasize developmental approaches to working with people, including attention to their cultural context and the influence of gender, race, age, ethnicity, sexual orientation, (dis)ability, and sociohistory (Fassinger, 1991, p. 172).

Over the more than 50 years of our organizational existence, our profession and the organizational representative of our profession (ACA) has evolved and changed with the times, but we have never changed our core values—of freedom, tolerance and acceptance, individual and collective responsibility, and of keeping humanity in all of our endeavors. I believe that we have the will to continue to do this and that we *can* do this, or I would not have spent a good 30 years of my professional life as a member of the counseling profession.

What is the next major societal transition, from technology to what, you may be asking? I have no idea, but what I do know is that professional counseling will be needed to help ease the pain in people's lives in that next transition, just as it has in the past and current ones. Our roots cause us to be in the forefront of helping people during societal transitions, of always advocating for and putting people first.

Those transitions from what-has-been to what-will-be have provided the major impetus for the growth of our profession and subsequent consolidation of that growth.

Let me leave you with this one final thought: the great philosopher Frederick Nietzsche in 1887 in his *Genealogy of Morals* said, "Every step forward is made at the cost of mental and physical pain to someone." (Ouch! Profound, but not very much fun.)

Our goal in professional counseling is to ease that pain of transition for all humanity and to keep humanity and the humane treatment of human beings in all that we do in our world. (See—there's that "human" word again.) It is a goal that we are well suited for. It is a goal that we embrace. It is a good goal, for it takes us back to our roots. Roots of change, social justice, social progress, and social advocacy. Keep that in mind as you go back to your workplaces and rejoice in our profession and the work that we do every day that makes this world a better place—one human being and one group at a time.

(*Noto fine:* Now, that wasn't too painful, was it? Thanks for staying with me. All the way to the end too. Applause to you.)

References

Aubrey, R. F. (1977). Historical development of guidance and counseling and implications for the future. *Personnel & Guidance Journal, 55,* 288–295.

Fassinger, R. E. (1991). The hidden minority: Issues and challenges in working with lesbian women and gay men. *The Counseling Psychologist, 19,* 157–176.

McDaniels, C. O. (1964). *The history and development of the American Personnel and Guidance Association 1952–1963.* Unpublished doctoral dissertation, The University of Virginia, Charlottesville, VA.

Pope, M. (2000). A brief history of career counseling in the USA. *The Career Development Quarterly, 48,* 194–211.

U. S. Census Bureau. (2000). *United States Census 2000.* Retrieved June 23, 2003, from http://www.census.gov/main/www/cen2000.html

Whiteley, J. (1984). *Counseling psychology: A historical perspective.* Schenectady, NY: Character Research Press.

Note: This chapter was originally an address titled "The Professional Counselor: Advancing the Profession by Returning to Our Roots" delivered at the Alabama Counseling Association Annual Convention on November 17, 2004, in Huntsville, AL.

Chapter 11

World Peace:
Another Laudable Goal

When you run for ACA President (or almost any elected position), you run on a platform that is composed of your goals. You know, the things you want to accomplish during your term of office.

Sometimes, such goals are like those of Miss America ("world peace"), and sometimes they are a bit too focused ("increase membership by 500"). Oh, by the way, neither of these goal statements is particularly bad. Hey, who wouldn't be for world peace or 500 more members?

Our goals this year are somewhere between those. Bear with me.

1. Provide primary and ongoing support to branches in their drive to achieve licensing in the few remaining states without LPCs or LMHCs—Hawaii, Nevada, and California.
2. Provide support (financial and technical) to branches that already have licensing, but are in need of refining and maintaining those gains.
3. Strengthen our legislative presence in Washington, DC, so that our hard-fought Congressional wins are preserved and expanded (like seeking to establish parity with other mental health professions for the reimbursement of services from public and nonpublic sources like Medicare and managed care); pass the 100,000 more school counselors legislation; and become more aggressive with managed care companies to ensure adequate client services and humane client treatment.
4. Establish a counseling specialties credential (diplomate) to meet the certification needs of divisions including school, career, gerontology, addictions, multicultural trainers, couples and family, mental health, and others.
5. Reassert our leadership among and collaborate with our sister organizations in the education and mental health fields including the American Psychological Association and the Counseling Psychology Division of APA, National School Boards Association, National Education Association, and National Association of Social Workers.

6. Secure our initial United Nation's status as a non-governmental organization (NGO) and insure our participation in and recognition by other international organizations—with the International Association for Counseling, the International Association for Educational and Vocational Guidance, the British Association for Counselling and Psychotherapy, and China's College Counseling Association.
7. Initiate leadership training in media and organizational relations at all levels of the Association to teach leaders how to successfully market the profession to external constituencies, like lawmakers, consumers, media, and other professional associations.
8. Continue to closely monitor our budget to secure our financial position.
9. Develop plans for an external government relations committee.
10. Increase focus on practice, client advocacy, and research at our annual convention.
11. And world peace.

The way I figure it, if we get 1 through 10, then 11 should fall into place pretty easily.

Note: This chapter was originally published as the "ACA President's Column" in the September 2003 issue of *Counseling Today*.

~~ Chapter 12

Politics: The Art of Building Relationships

First, I need to warn you. Along with my advanced degrees in counseling, I have a degree in political science too. I even went to law school for a while (please don't hate me). My first elected political office was Parliamentarian of the Fisk-Rombauer (MO) High School Library Club (I don't count my election to "prince" in the fourth grade) and, with a fast start like that, you can see that I was headed for political greatness. (Having fun?) My father ran for County Assessor once and my stepfather ran for State Senator once. Both lost; therefore, I am the most successful political person in the history my family. (Stay with me, I'm getting to my point.)

I am perplexed.

Two of the primary competencies of our profession are communication and the relationship. We are the experts in defining, analyzing, and categorizing human communication—direct or indirect, verbal or nonverbal. It's a closed-end question or it's an interpretation statement. It's what we do. It's who we are.

We are also quite able to do the same with relationships whether it's an individual counseling relationship, a group, or a family system. We know that the power of counseling lies in the relationship. And we are even trained to analyze the cultural context of individuals and their relationships. It's what we do. It's who we are. We are the experts.

During my academic and experiential training in political science (and, while I am on the subject, why do they call it political "science" when both the theory and the practice of politics is truly an "art"?), I learned that the skills that make one successful in politics are also the skills of communication and relationship. Our exact professional skills!

Politics is simply the art of building relationships. To be a successful "public policy influencer," you are merely building a relationship with a political leader and his or her staff. It's all about having a message and communicating it effectively and building a relationship so that they will discount neither you nor your message. See, it's a lot easier for Senator Bill Frist of Tennessee, the US Senate Majority Leader, to send a form letter to a nameless, faceless constituent than it is for him to send the same letter to Ms. Nita Jones of Dyersburg, TN, a school counselor, a leader of the Tennessee School Counselors Association and Tennessee Counseling Association, a National Education Association Board member, and the ACA Southern Region Chair, whom he has now met personally on numerous occasions, and from whom he has received donations, a Christmas card, family pictures, and issue letters on a quite regular basis. (It's hard to ignore Nita!) She has used her personal and professional skills to successfully build a "relationship."

So, wouldn't you be perplexed too that, when it comes to politics, the large majority of us are, at best, ineffective or, at worst, just plain absent. Now don't get me wrong, there are some of us who are very good at this. But for most of us, we don't pay much attention to politics, except when it hurts us economically or touches our lives in (what we perceive as) negative ways ("They're gonna cut our reimbursement rate from $60 per hour to $5?"). Even then, there is a bit of resignation in us that impels us to just accept (what we perceive as) "the inevitable." "You can't fight City Hall!" (The exclamation point there is out of place as there is no such energy in that kind of statement, merely acceptance.) "What can one person really do?" Our President-Elect Sam Gladding might have quoted in a speech (he often quotes song lyrics, you know) the Crosby, Stills, Nash, and Young lyric, "We are helpless, helpless, helpless, helplesssss." Sad, isn't it? Not Sam or his lyrical quoting, but the idea that we are all helpless and can have no effect on what the government (or any large bureaucracy) does "to" us.

But, hell, I'm not helpless! (appropriate exclamation point) One person's voice can make a difference, and a whole lot of professional counselors' voices speaking in unison about a single message not only can, but does, make a difference. With 60,000 voices around the world asking for the inclusion of professional counselors in the Medicare law, we can be heard and make a difference!

Now, I know that you may be feeling that we are applying our professional skills in a different way than politicians do—we are trying to help humanity. But, let me tell you something, many who are in "public service" also believe that is what they are trying to do, too. Now, those who are of a more cynical persuasion doubt it. They think that all politicians are just in it for power and money. Some are (alas). But not all are. (I need to believe this.) And, anyway, no matter what they are in it for, we need their votes on our issues and we need to be there, fighting passionately for truth and justice, for the good of our profession (guild issues), as well as for the good of our clients and their/our world (social justice issues).

And we are doing some exceptional work. This year we have marshalled our forces to invade Capitol Hill more often (colorful language, eh?). Each year, we have a National Legislative Institute in February where state and national leaders receive further training on how to use their natural and expert skills in communication and relationship building for the good of our profession. During that institute, we spend several days training our people and then we take them to the Hill to exercise these skills (it's kind of like practicum followed by a supervised field experience). Then, this past November at our

National Branch and Leadership Training Academy in Washington, DC, we also took over 70 of our state counseling leaders from 20 states to Capitol Hill to meet with their US Senators and members of Congress on three critical issues for our profession: (1) reauthorization of the Workforce Investment Act (WIA); (2) reauthorization of the Elementary and Secondary School Counselor Program (ESSCP); and (3) amending the Medicare law to include recognition and reimbursement of members of our profession (we are soooooo close). Third, we have a new subcommittee of our Public Policy and Legislation Committee that is working on selected social justice issues from our Legislative Agenda. That subcommittee is composed of graduate students in counseling at George Mason University in Virginia, supervised by Dr. Rita Chung, who serves on our Human Rights Committee. We are very proud of the work that we are doing.

We in ACA are committed to informing our membership on these issues and all of the others that regularly arise at both the national and state levels. We have a public policy staff of four now (Scott Barstow, Dara Alpert, Chris Campbell, and Christie Lum) and other executive staff members (Richard Yep, Executive Director, and Janice Macdonald, Special Projects Director) who are former Congressional staff members.

But I am here to tell you that even this is not enough. We are entering the primary election season leading up to the November 2004 general election of a new President and a new Congress, new governors and new state legislatures, and new school boards. So now I have another assignment for you. (I am trying to be sensitive to your busy schedules here, but this is important!) Just like you are now doing with the "marketing the profession" assignment (refresher in the October *Counseling Today*), I want you to use your natural, expert counseling skills to develop a relationship with your members of Congress, Governor, State Representative, school board member—you pick. Think about how you would like to be approached if you were in a similar position and then just do it. If you need any materials (research, policy statements, addresses, etc.), you can contact Scott Barstow, our Director of Public Policy at ACA headquarters (sbarstow@counseling.org) and he will get you anything you want. He's a good guy.

And you also ought to know about the Professional Counseling Fund, a political action committee that was formed by a bunch of eminent leaders of our profession. You can get info on them at www.counselingfund.org.

Bottomline: Since you are an expert at counseling, then you could be good at politics too since each has similar skill sets. You just have to see the need (protect your job and/or world peace, whatever gets you through the night) and make it a higher priority. Politics is simply the art of relationship building, and you've got all the right stuff! (another appropriate exclamation point)

And also, don't forget to vote in our own ACA elections. I assure you that it is more important than you think.

Note: Portions of this chapter were originally published as the "ACA President's Column" in the December 2003 issue of *Counseling Today*.

Chapter 13

Professional Development: It's What Makes Us All True Professionals

Through my columns as your President, I have told you about myself and my Mom to get you to care more about our profession. I have talked about professional identity. I have pleaded with you to market our profession more boldly. I have told you about the life of one of our most revered members who died in 2004 (Mary Arnold). I have reported on social justice issues that affect our gay, lesbian, and bisexual clients. I have tried to engage you in your profession. Now I want to ask you to do one more thing. (I find the word "thing" so . . . utilitarian.)

This particular chapter is about a very practical issue: your professional development.

First, let's review what it takes to be a "professional." Here's a good definition: of or pertaining to a profession or calling; conforming to the rules or standards of a profession; following a profession, as professional knowledge or professional conduct. A profession, then, is often restricted to include only those occupations requiring extensive study and possessing a specialized knowledge or theory base, such as counseling, education, medicine, nursing, law, or engineering.

(George Bernard Shaw, in one of his more curmudgeonly moods, characterized all professions as "conspiracies against the laity." And, although I have an appreciation for Mr. Shaw's definition, let's smile but not dawdle.)

Today, I want to focus on the "professional knowledge or conduct" piece of this. You get your first dose of this in your graduate training. In this training you get the basics, the foundation upon which your professionalism rests. When we who are counselor educators are convinced that you have achieved a basic competence in knowledge and skills, we allow you to go forward. We certify to the world that you are a professional counselor by awarding you an advanced graduate degree. You can place that certificate of graduation on your wall to let those who seek your services know that you have achieved such professional training. (In that way you are already very special. Only 5.5% of all the people in the US have a master's degree or higher.)

But you also have other professional responsibilities that begin with your entry into our profession. Joining and participating in our professional associations (American Counseling Association and our Divisions, Organizational Affiliates, and Branches). Obeying the ethical code of our profession. Following the laws and policies under which you are credentialed. Maintaining professional liability insurance. And a very important part of being a professional is keeping current about the practice of our profession. We call the last one "professional development."

The true bottomline is that you can't be a professional unless you keep current in your profession. It is not enough to get a degree and then drop off of the face of the professional world. You have responsibilities to belong and keep current.

Counseling means change. (Radical!) The question for me as a professional counselor is how to be the most effective agent for change. And in order to be effective, you need tools. You get tools through professional development. ACA provides opportunities to keep current and manage your professional development.

Back in 1974 when I attended my first professional counseling convention (ACA was called the American Personnel and Guidance Association then), I was only 22 years old and trying to figure out this professional thing. I had a *great* time at the convention. I was an M.Ed. student at the University of Missouri–Columbia and a lot of my professors were going and so I thought that was what you were supposed to do. So, I went. And, I loved it!

I met a lot of new people from all over the US and the world. I learned so much from the workshops that I attended. I went to some meetings (yes, even at that young age, I was already attending "meetings"). I got to hear, see, and even sometimes meet some of the people who wrote my textbooks and who were legends to me—Carl Rogers, Albert Ellis, and many others.

It was a very powerful event in my professional life. Sure, I also had one night at the convention when I had a little too much fun (you know, "wine, men, song," those sorts of things). (I have since learned better "convention behavior management skills.") But, it was a "peak experience" (see Maslow) of my professional life.

Then, I got a chance as ACA President to design "My Perfect Convention," which occurred in Kansas City, April 2004. Just think about what you would like to see at your perfect convention. Well, here was my plan.

On the first day of the convention, our opening keynote address was a panel of multicultural counseling experts talking about the progress in combating prejudice that we have made in our profession and in the country during the 50 years since the US Supreme Court handed down one of its most important rulings in Brown v. The Board of Education of Topeka, Kansas. I asked Courtland Lee, one of our most distinguished ACA Past-Presidents, to lead this lustrous panel discussion with Miguel Arciniega, Anita Jackson, Judy Lewis, and Michael Hutchins. It was a must-see celebration of what has been accomplished since that historic ruling and of what remains to be accomplished for our clients, our society, and our world.

On the second day, the convention opened with a Living Legends panel of Albert Ellis, William Glasser, Patricia Arredondo, John Krumboltz, and Jon Carlson. It was also a celebration of Dr. Ellis's 90th birthday. It is one of the reasons that we all come to such conventions—to see the pioneers and legends of our profession and to be motivated by seeing them one more time. I still remember the times that I saw Carl Rogers, B. F. Skinner, and Virginia Satir.

We also had a town hall meeting on our new revised ethical code; the largest and most professional exhibition hall seen in years; a different format for and even more poster sessions; more applied research than we ever had before to inform everyday practice; a focus on social justice, culture, and relationship building; the first Hans Z. Hoxter International Forum; and dancers from the Haskell Indian Nations University in nearby Lawrence, Kansas. And we moved the big party to the opening night with a *Wizard of Oz* theme. Wow! (Okay, so I was over the top on this one, but it was really good.)

Attendees also got to meet my brother, Doug, as he opened the convention with a Cherokee purification ceremony and my partner Mario.

When you're ACA President, the convention is a physical, emotional, interpersonal, and political marathon, as you go from three days of Governing Council meetings (that you prepare, preside over, and hope it all works out ok), to a day of ACA Committee meetings where you go to each meeting and bring greetings and thank-you's for a job well done and congratulations to the new members, to three more days of opening sessions, more meetings, receptions, hand-shaking, people-hugging, and baby-kissing. I felt like I was in a "make nice, be friends, play together" boot camp during that entire week. I was averaging about four hours of sleep a night. Not eating very much. Not drinking adult beverages very much. Getting up at 4:30 a.m. checking my prepared remarks, reviewing my schedule for that day, doing my exercises, and keeping myself centered and present. (It takes a lot of work to look spontaneous. I told you that my "convention behavior management skills" have improved.) And, loving it, loving every single moment of every minute of it!

So, how did it turn out? The weather was magnificent. Kansas City was magnificent. The convention facilities were magnificent. The exposition hall was sold out. The hotels were sold out. The steak and barbeque were scrumptious, an Atkins delight. The programs were truly outstanding. The opening session was emotional from the beginning to the end. The Living Legends session was memorable as Albert Ellis serenaded us and as we serenaded him by singing "happy birthday" on his 90th birthday.

Some other important but less obvious events also happened at our convention that I thought you'd like to hear about. These all have to do with marketing our profession and educating others about who we are and what we do. I would like all of us to just make nice and be friends and play together. (Note that this as a recurring theme in my life. I'm pretty sure that it's something that my Mom and Dad did to me at a very early age.)

Leaders of the American Association of Marriage and Family Therapy attended our convention. The editor of *The Counseling Psychologist* attended our convention and met with all the ACA and our Division journal editors.

The Professional Counseling Fund held its inaugural reception and raised $5,000. The Professional Counseling Fund is a new political action committee formed this year.

Three international professional counseling associations were in attendance at our convention. Leaders of the International Association for Counselling, the Canadian Counselling Association, and the British Association for Counselling and Psychotherapy were honored during our opening session as well as at the first International Leaders Tea.

And finally, one of my goals had been to keep us all together. And two of our very important (*all* are very important) Divisions over this past year strengthened their ties to ACA. The American School Counselor Association and the American Mental Health Counselor Association never left, but they had been drifting farther away organizationally and politically over the past 10 years. The move at last year's ACA Governing Council meeting in Anaheim to begin a charter revocation process sparked a yearlong process of discussion and reconciliation. There were some pretty high-level discussions occurring, including special trips to Florida and Arkansas to conduct a little face-to-face diplomacy. A lot of the credit has to go to the presidents and governing boards that began to develop a more "we" professional identity and some more trust. It has not been an easy process, but it has been a gratifying process. There are still differences, but it seems to me that the attitude has changed and we are now beginning to focus on our similarities rather than our differences as well as the positives rather than the negatives —much better places from which to collaborate. Thank you especially to Gail Adams (AMHCA President) and Russ Sabella (ASCA President) for their professionalism and leadership.

My Mom sends her regrets as she wasn't able to get to Kansas City this time (she's not doing too well these days), but she sent my brother Doug to stand in for her and my other brothers. Doug led the Native American purification ritual (what we call "smudging") during the opening session with a hardy band of Native counselors assisting: Roger Herring (Lumbee), Tarrell Portman (Cherokee), John Peregoy (Flathead), and Kelley Kenny (Cherokee).

My partner Mario was also at the opening session, and being able to introduce him was very special. It has been reported to me by what I consider reliable sources that there was not a dry eye in the house during that part of the opening session, including mine. Yeah, I'm a very emotional, committed, and passionate person, and it has taken a special person to put up with me for the past eight years. I love him very much.

And I even got a beautiful Hawaiian lei and the Ohana Award (from Counselors for Social Justice via Judy Lewis) in the middle of the ACA Awards

Ceremony, a Lakota Sioux peace medal from our Association for Spiritual, Ethical, and Religious Values in Counseling (via Bruce Dickinson), the first Cesar Chavez Servicio a Otros (Service to Others) Award from our Association for Multicultural Counseling and Development (via Robert Davison-Aviles), a bottle of Bombay Sapphire Gin from Deneen Pennington, Executive Director of the National Career Development Association, and a spontaneous standing ovation from my brothers and sisters in our Association for Gay, Lesbian, and Bisexual Issues in Counseling when I walked into their brunch (very moving). All in all a very satisfying time.

See what a good time you can have as you develop yourself professionally. ACA is our professional home that meets so many of our professional development needs. Make sure you get to the next ACA Convention. I'm willing to bet that you will also find yourself positively addicted. It's pretty heady stuff. See you at the next convention. Make sure you come up and introduce yourself and give me a hug. You (er, I) can never get enough hugs!

Note: Portions of this chapter were originally titled "Springtime for ACA in Kansas City" and "Make Nice, Be Friends, and Play Together" and published as the "ACA President's Column" in the March 2004 and May 2004 issues of *Counseling Today,* respectively.

━━Chapter 14

So You Want to Be a Leader: Top 10 (or so) Habits of Effective Leaders

My first elective office was Library Club Parliamentarian at the Fisk-Rombauer (MO) High School (65 people in my graduating class of 1969). (A very fast start, eh?) In the counseling profession, I have also been elected to numerous positions, the highlights of which are the 52nd President of the American Counseling Association (ACA), the 80th President of the National Career Development Association (NCDA), and the third male co-chair of the National Caucus of Gay and Lesbian Counselors (the predecessor of the ACA Division, the Association of Gay, Lesbian, and Bisexual Issues in Counseling; AGLBIC). In between these elected positions, I have also done a lot of other work that I will not go into here. Suffice it to say that you don't get elected to do these jobs without paying your dues over an entire career.

I have some friends who say that my life is inspirational. I say they are crazy (not a professional judgment, just a general observation). I just do my job. This chapter is dedicated to the next generation of leaders in professional counseling who are "just doing their jobs."

This chapter is about becoming a leader, both the objective part as well as the subjective. Generally, I think these attributes are true of all leaders of most everything, but here I'll focus on professional counseling because we are a little different (you knew that). I grew up in the 1960s and, as a victim of the times, was one of those people who wanted to change the world. Actually, that formulation is not exactly correct. I have *always* wanted to change the world, to make it a just and safe and peace-filled place. The 1960s just gave me a broader stage upon which to play and to further develop that philosophy.

I'm writing about the "habits" because it's something you do over and over and it becomes ingrained, almost like a personality trait early formed (e.g., extraversion). I've been studying the history of our profession and the players in that history for many years. Here's what I've observed about my colleagues who see service to our profession as an important part of their career (read, "life").

Also, let me be clear: I do not necessarily have all of these habits, or, if I do have some, I have them in varying degrees or use them with varying degrees of success.

The Objective

So what does it take to be a good leader in the counseling profession? Here's my top 10 list. Okay, so it's a little longer than 10, but you get my drift. (By the way, when I say "you must have" in the following list, I mean "develop or already have" and I mean this to be a guide, not really a "must." It will sound presumptuous, but it is not meant that way. I just want these to give you some ideas of what might be useful to you in your leadership roles.) I hope you are enjoying this.

1. First and most importantly, you must have a passion for our profession. Not any two-bit, temporary, buy it today and sell it tomorrow, watch it go down the drain without doing something kind of passion. But a full-force, love it, believe in it, I'm here for all time, I can't imagine not doing this, I found my life's calling kind of passion. Real genuine passion.
2. You must also have a vision; you must see our path clearly and be able to motivate others toward your vision.
3. You must persist, even knowing that you may fail (on more than one occasion).
4. You must have a thick skin, but thin enough to still feel both the highs and the pain.
5. You must have perspective and common sense.
6. You must be able to ask for help, especially from the right people. You know, mentors. You must have some and use them wisely.
7. You must love humanity, in all its various manifestations and variations, honoring diversity in all things.
8. You must also have an edge—willing to take a strong stand and yet willing to compromise as appropriate.
9. You must have a love of the history of the profession and know the difference we have made in society.
10. You must have personal humility while at the same time singing the praises of our profession consistently, unremittingly, and tirelessly.
11. You must have a sense of humor and use it responsibly and at the appropriate time.
12. You must have respect. Respect for our elders, our institutions, our headquarters staff, our colleagues, and our profession.
13. You must have the political skills of collaboration, communication, and negotiation.
14. You must value differences. Note that this is not always easy, especially when someone disagrees with your own core values.

15. You must always balance process and outcome. I am an outcome guy, but many of your colleagues are process people. You need both to be successful. Our group counseling friends will tell us that a good process is just as important as a good outcome. Okay, so they're right (especially in our profession), but I really hate for them to hear that coming from me.
16. You must enjoy meetings (or at least tolerate them very well).
17. You must have a life partner who loves you and is willing to take up the slack at home when you are gone to another one of those meetings.
18. You must have integrity and do what you do for the good of the profession, not yourself. Giving back without expecting reward is a critical component of a life of service. If you expect rewards and honors, you will be frustrated by your expectations. Go for the intrinsic rewards instead.

Okay, I think I'm about listed out and I can already hear you crying "enough," so I will stop.

The Subjective

I've given you the objective part of this; now for the subjective. I wanted to title this section "My Life," but, with apologies to Leon Trotsky and Bill Clinton, it's been rather overused. I think that in general this next section is more fun.

Back in the early 1970s when I was a newbie in our profession, I met three men who changed my life. Those three men were John McGowan, Bob Callis, and Norm Gysbers—all three were my professors in the Department of Counseling and Personnel Services in the College of Education at the University of Missouri–Columbia.

Let me give you a little career background for context.

I was a senior at the University of Missouri–Columbia majoring in political science and sociology and headed for law school, followed surely by US Senator from Missouri and, eventually, President of the United States. As a product of the 1960s, the anti–Vietnam War movement, President Nixon's invasion of Cambodia, and the killing of protesting students at Jackson State University and at Kent State University, I had helped lead a student and faculty strike that had shut down our campus at the end of 1970. Ah, the good old days.

Then I had become involved in student government and was elected student body vice-president at the end of my sophomore year in college. Along with a cabal of like-minded student politicos, we took over the student government and ran it for the next five years—The Individual Coalition Party—a coalition of individuals seeking our rights as students in an unfair and unjust system—the university. I was headed for law school, but found through my involvement in student government that I was exposed to "student personnel work." I had never heard of nor considered a career in this area in my whole life. When I was growing up, I first wanted to be a cowperson, followed by physician, eventually narrowed to pediatrician, but after extensive career counseling at the Testing & Counseling Center with Prentice Gautt (a doctoral student in counseling and ex–running back for the St. Louis Cardinals) and receiving my results from my Strong Vocational Interest Blank, I had decided that law was my goal and political science was my path. I wanted to be a civil rights attorney (not corporate or criminal—civil rights) and help the downtrodden masses. I was headed for law school when (I believe that Maslow calls these incidents "peak experiences," as they change the course of your life) the assistant to the Chancellor at the university sat me down one day and told me that I should not waste all of the experience and knowledge that I had gained through my service in student government. He said that I should think about making a career in the student affairs area and told me that most people who worked in that area got their master's degree in Counseling and Student Personnel Services and, lucky me, we had one of the top programs in the country right in our own backyard. I had never considered it, but I was immediately intrigued. I thought about it a while and, instead of applying directly to law school, I applied to graduate school in Counseling and Student Personnel Services to get my master's degree.

I was assigned Dr. Robert Callis as my advisor, and he scared me. He was a tall, swarthy University of Minnesota grad who had been Dean of Students on our campus a while ago and had authored or coauthored several psychological inventories. He had lots of doctoral students but only three of us who were his master's students. He had a long history of involvement in both professional counseling and counseling psychology, and he had been president of the American College Personnel Association (one of the founding Divisions of the American Counseling Association) as well as holding an office and several leadership positions in Division 17 (the Counseling Psychology Division of the American Psychological Association).

Then, there was Dr. John McGowan, who was a Creighton University grad. During my undergraduate career, I had served as one of two student members on the Chancellor Search Committee. Dr. McGowan was the Dean of Extension then, a very powerful position at a state, land-grant university. I had become very close to Dr. McGowan. He became my friend and mentor, and I blame much of what has transpired since then on him. He too was a faculty member in Counseling and Student Personnel Services and he also had held important leadership positions in our profession including President of Division 17.

Then, during my first semester in my master's program, I was required to take Occupational and Educational Information ("Occ & Ed," as it was lovingly referred to by those of us who were being forced to take it. Hey, we thought, we'll never need this career counseling stuff—this is only amusing when you remember that I later went on to be president of the National Career Development Association). That course was taught by Dr. Norm Gysbers, who was a graduate of the University of Michigan. I found out that he had been President of the National Career Development Association and then later President of the American Counseling Association.

I was impressed. Three of my professors were not just exceptional professors but they were also leaders in the counseling profession. The message that I got from them was that it was your responsibility to be involved in your profession through service in your professional associations. This is a lesson that I have taken to heart (according to my partner Mario, too much so). All three felt a responsibility to belong, but much more than belong, to help lead our whole profession. And they saw the profession as broader than one association, one kind of degree, or one anything. They felt a responsibility for where we were heading at all levels of our profession. This has had a profound effect on my developing professional identity.

Then, I also began to come to grips with my amodal sexual orientation. Okay, so this was something that I had been trying to cope with for a while. I had tried to get out of it by marrying my high school sweetheart. By bargaining with myself that I could not be gay because I wanted children. By talking to my local Presbyterian minister, who told me that I was going to hell, etc. As you probably know by now, this did not turn out to be a strategy that was effective in the long run.

However, with the acceptance of my gay identity came a whole host of other realizations including that I was probably not going to be President of the US. Hey, call me crazy, but in 1973, it did not exactly look like this career path had a high probability of success. So I began to focus my political work toward changing the view of my new profession on issues of sexual orientation.

I attended my first ACA Convention while studying for my master's degree. I met Dr. Joe Norton, who had founded the Caucus of Gay Counselors in ACA, and I was hooked. My emerging professional identity and cultural identity had found a home—together. It was too much to ask.

I became the third male chair of the Caucus of Gay Counselors in ACA with Dr. Ann Strack (a University of Missouri–Columbia grad too, by the way). We changed our name during our term to the National Caucus of Gay and Lesbian Counselors.

Later, I moved to San Francisco for love (he dumped me later), but I stayed in San Francisco and became involved with the California Career Development Association. I had been involved in career counseling for many years, and I have a passion for career work. I was also working for Consulting Psychologists Press at that time and completing my doctoral work at the University of San Francisco in the Department of Counseling and Educational Psychology.

I worked my way up through the ranks of the California Career Development Association until I was elected President in 1993–1994. One of the things that I have learned is that, if you show you are interested, volunteer, work hard, and follow through, you will get a good reputation as a leader and others will ask you to take on more responsibility. This is also a good strategy for life, I have found.

Later, David Jepsen, at the University of Iowa, who was the immediate Past-President of the National Career Development Association and chairing the nominations and elections committee of that professional association, asked me to run for an office in NCDA. I was elected secretary and served for two years, then treasurer for three years, and then President of NCDA in 1998–1999. That office is probably the office that I am most proud of because of the very important place that NCDA has in the history of our profession. Founded in 1913 as the National Vocational Guidance Association, its list of presidents reads like a who's who of our profession (Donald Super, Ed Herr, Sunny Hansen, Norm Gysbers, Ken Hoyt, Jane Goodman, Lee Richmond, and many others).

Then, in 2002 I was elected President of the American Counseling Association, following Donald Super by exactly 50 years—he was the second ACA President and I am the 52nd. I am proud of this for many reasons, not the least of which is that I have always followed my mentors in the profession—Callis, McGowan, and Gysbers—who saw themselves as bridges to both professional counseling and counseling psychology. I proudly carry that banner. Each enriches the other.

Lavender Ceilings

I need to do some definitional work here before I proceed. In this chapter I specifically mention a "lavender ceiling." Some of you may know what this is, but others may not. Please bear with me. This term comes from the industrial and organizational psychology and business literature and is a variation of the phrase "the glass ceiling." That image was first used as a symbol of an invisible barrier between middle management and top management that women could never get through because of their gender. Later this was expanded to include race, ethnicity, sexual orientation, physical disability, or whatever makes you different from the dominant group of that culture and is used as a barrier to your ever achieving membership in the top leadership echelon of that institution, be it a business or a professional association. It is there. It stops your advancement. But you never really see it.

If you coat the glass in the ceiling with a light purple color before you install it, you then get a lavender tint. The origins of the term lavender vary from: (1) a color associated with gay men since Ancient Greece, where the Greek word for lavender also meant a gay man; (2) the custom in sixteenth century England in which both men and women indicated that they did not intend to marry by wearing violets; (3) a mixture of blue (traditional color for males) and pink (traditional color for females), thereby creating a fusion of genders; two-spirited or twin-spirited person is a native American term for GLBT persons; (4) a blending of women and men, a oneness that makes a special kind of community; or (5) the color combination of the pink triangle that gay men were forced to wear in concentration camps in Nazi Germany and the black triangle that Nazis used to identify "socially unacceptable" women—lesbians were included in that classification.

The term "lavender" is in general usage by GLBT groups, including the Lavender Dragon Society (a group of GLBT Asians), Lavender Languages Conferences (a conference on the lexicon of GLBT community), the Lavender Youth Recreation and Information Center (a GLBT youth center in San Francisco).

The term lavender ceiling was not used officially, however, until 1996 when a group of researchers (Friskopp, & Silverstein, 1995) applied the term to the inability of GLBT employees to fully enjoy career development and promotional advancement because they are, or are perceived to be, GLBT. Based on a Harvard Business School study, their book was a candid examination of the working lives of America's gays and lesbians. Men and women at every career stage and across the professional spectrum talked frankly about coming out in the workplace, harassment, discrimination, and the persistence of the lavender ceiling. The authors identified the lavender ceiling, homophobia, and heterosexism as issues that impact both the emotional and financial well-being of GLBT employees.

Now, applying this to ACA at the time I was elected in 2002, there had only been 53 people elected to the ACA presidency and 90 to the NCDA Presidency. I have compiled the demographics for the ACA Presidents just to give you a flavor.

- Males 31 (58.5%)
- Females 22 (41.5%)
- 15 (93.8%) of the first 16 presidents were male
- 12 (75%) of the last 16 were female
- 3 (5.7%) of the 53 were African American
- 0 were Asian
- 0 were Hispanic
- One was Native American
- One was openly gay (at least 4 that I know of were sexual minorities by the way, but it is not my purpose to out them here)
- One had a major physical disability (a congenital birth defect called spina bifida, which means I have bone missing from my spinal column that makes for an unstable back and leads to easy injury, mobility problems, and a certain level of chronic pain—by the way, this is merely data, not a complaint. My mother complains, I merely provide data.)

Those last three statistics were me.

Breaking into such a small group takes perseverance, hard work, a vision, some talent, and luck. There have only been a very few openly gay or lesbian leaders who have been able to attain these offices in the counseling professions. I was the first "openly" gay man and first Native American to be elected to either the NCDA or ACA presidency.

I know that all of us who are professional counselors have a passion for our profession and the work that we do. We love counseling and believe in the good we do in the world or else we just wouldn't do it. We want to help others.

We see the power of counseling to create positive change in people's lives, and by extension, the world. And, we are in our profession for the long run.

I learned from my mentors that, when I entered our profession, I automatically had some new responsibilities—professional responsibilities. When you receive your graduate degree in our profession, you take on these professional responsibilities. There is nothing you can do about it. It's there. It's inherent in your new status. Along with your membership in our profession, it has now become your responsibility as a professional counselor to give something back to your profession. This is a responsibility that you will now have—everyday of your life, as long as you live, work, or breathe. It is a huge responsibility. And it is a responsibility not just to your profession, but also to your family and friends, to your community and to the society in which we live, because our profession touches everything and makes profound differences in the quality of life at every level—from the personal to societal.

Belonging to the American Counseling Association and providing leadership to our profession ensures the continuation of our profession. Ensures that counseling or whatever it is that we evolve into, continues to help others and remind others (in all daily activities) of our humanity. It is our professional responsibility, but even more, it is what we *must* do.

Each of *you* is why I am so committed to our profession and why I have chosen to do this work. I think that we are truly blessed to have found our profession and that is why I want us to prosper, grow, and be able reach every person in the world who so desperately needs our help. I believe so very passionately in counseling, in the good that we do in the world. Freud talked about "love and work" as the hallmarks of the mature life. I count myself among the lucky ones in this world, for I have found what I love in my life, it is mine—my partner Mario, my big inclusive family, my friends, and my even bigger professional family.

Thank you for caring about our profession and for allowing me to serve you. I invite you into the leadership of professional counseling. I hope that I have provided some insight into one leader's journey. Also, as the first openly gay president of a major mental health professional association and as a Native American, I hope that my story and observations may inspire other members of racial, ethnic, sexual, or other minorities to more fully participate in the leadership of our profession. And finally, if this moves even one future ACA president toward a path of professional service, it has all been worth it. It has truly been a labor of love.

Reference

Friskopp, A., & Silverstein, S. (1995). *Straight jobs, gay lives*. NY: Scribner.

Note: Portions of this chapter were originally presented as an invited lecture at Kent State University in Kent, Ohio, sponsored by their Chi Sigma Iota chapter, in October 2003.

Chapter 15

You've Just Got to Have Standards:
On Licensing, Ethics, Certification,
and Accreditation

Hello once again. I'm in Stratford-upon-Avon, Will Shakespeare's home, attending the British Association for Counseling and Psychotherapy's annual convention. They are treating me quite nicely, but the little place we are staying in doesn't know how to make a good martini (rats!).

During 2005, the 48th state in the USA achieved licensing for its professional counselors (Question: last two? Answer: California and Nevada). Kudos to Hawaii and to the ACA members in Hawaii who made it happen! I was at an international symposium on career development when I received this important news. Many ACA presidents note the achievement of licensing for professional counselors in a specific state as an accomplishment during their term of office. (David Kaplan—ACA President before me—got New York. I got Hawaii. Yes!)

You might be asking why this is so important. Why do we make such a big deal about this? Well, actually, we make a big deal about licensing, and ethics, and certification, and accreditation, because they are the "Big 4" in defining a profession. It all falls under the rubric of "professional standards."

Let me do some quick definitional work for those of you unschooled in the esoterica of professions in the USA.

"Licensing" is where a state passes laws and develops regulations to define a profession and protect the consumers of the services of that profession. For example, in Missouri we have Licensed Professional Counselors that are regulated by a state governmental agency called the Missouri Committee for Professional Counselors. In other states they may be called Licensed Mental Health Counselors like in New York, or Licensed Clinical Professional Counselors like in Illinois.

"Ethics" are the agreed upon standards for self-regulation of a profession developed by a professional association. In 2005, a new *ACA Code of Ethics* was approved by the American Counseling Association after three years of discussion and debate among the membership (American Counseling Association, 2005).

"Certification" is where a national (sometimes state) body develops a list of minimum requirements for the effective and appropriate practice of a profession and certifies to the world that certain individuals have met those foundational requirements. For example, the National Board for Certified Counselors (NBCC) certifies counselors for general practice (NCC) or for some specialty practices (NCSC or CDF), or the Commission on Rehabilitation Counselor Certification (CRCC) that certified rehabilitation counselors (CRC) or even the National Career Development Association that certifies master career counselors (MCC) and master career development professionals (MCDP) or the International Association of Marriage and Family Counselors that certifies couples, marriage, and family counselors (CFT).

"Acccreditation" is where a national body develops a list of minimum requirements for the effective and appropriate training of new professionals and accredits certain colleges and universities who meet their requirements. For example, the Council for Accreditation of Counseling and Related Educational Programs (CACREP) accredits programs in school counseling, community counseling, career counseling, mental health counseling, and others. The Council on Rehabilitation Education (CORE) accredits programs in rehabilitation counseling.

These four are *critical* for all of us who are professional counselors. So that we can be recognized as service providers in the mental health and education and labor arenas—anywhere professional counselors practice our profession.

The recognition of a profession is not simply a one-time event. There is no one who waves a magic wand and suddenly we are all *professional*. This is an ongoing struggle for all professions—whether they are professional counselors, or psychiatrists, or psychologists, or social workers, or nurses, or barbers (er, hair stylists).

Professions have a life and go through stages in their professional identity development. In the beginning you have ... the beginning. "It began as a mere twinkle in someone's eye." We attribute the founding of our profession to Professor Frank Parsons back in Boston, but the truth is that there were a whole bunch of people who were active and working with Professor Parsons. People such as Meyer Bloomfield and Jesse B. Davis and Ralph Albertson and Pauline Agassiz Shaw and Frank Leavitt and John Brewer.

Then you have the growth period where everyone wants to join and be a part of this new movement, followed by the maintenance period after the rush of growth. This is the most dangerous period. Because this is where a profession can lose it—can lose their way. It is a time of consolidation of the gains of the new growth. If you have good visionary leadership and a membership that has a passion for your existence and is willing to change to meet the new needs of a society, then you continue. But, if you lose your zeal or passion or ability to change, you die. Quickly sometimes, lingering sometimes, but you die a sure death and your profession ceases to be. Dead.

It is true that, at a certain point historically, some professions just die out. (We call them "dinosaurs" because we think that dinosaurs died out because they were unable to change when dramatic environmental changes occurred.) It is just the natural evolution of things (probably not in Kansas, but everywhere else—sorry, Kansas.) Professions that die out all have one thing in common—they don't change with the times. We, as a profession, are pretty good at changing with the times, but not perfect. I wrote a while back in a journal article that the growth of counseling is spurred by societal transitions. You know, it's the "were changing from an agrarian to an industrial society" thing and we need more machinists than farmers, and we need more people in urban areas than in rural areas. And we especially need more counselors to help people cope with all the changes during a social transition. Societies and people and professions change to meet the new needs of a new time or, if they don't, they die.

Let me assure you that we are not dying. We are alive and well and moving forward. We have made great leaps forward in the last 50 years. But we can never be complacent with our success, because there are always those out there who would like to see us go away, or become like nursing assistants (certified nursing assistants, but still assistants).

And that is why ACA exists. It's like when you hold a copyright on a book or a trademark on a special logo. If you don't try to protect your copyright or your trademark from others who might use it, then it becomes worthless, meaningless—so say the courts. If you do not try to enforce your trademark's uniqueness, the courts have said that you lose the rights to it. That is one of ACA's main purposes for being—to enforce our rights as members of a profession to exist and to practice what we have been trained to do.

ACA, our Divisions, and our Branches are the developers and enforcers of our standards as a profession.

When you are ACA President, one of the most important duties that you perform is to respond to irate members (it's not particularly fun, but it is important). I got this e-mail one day from a member:

> I've been asked to renew my membership, but I doubt that I will. Said constructively and without malice: I've been a member for over a decade. In that time I can honestly say that I am not aware of a single benefit from that rather costly membership.
>
> No laws have changed that benefit my practice. The insurance industry continues to not recognized our profession. Reciprocity is still a dream that seems far, far away. The liability insurance issue was a hassle, to include one of your "preferred and recommended" companies now notifying us that they will not be renewing our policies. Maybe I'm ignorant to the work that's ongoing, but I have nothing tangible after more than a decade of membership.
>
> You may be the one who changes ACA's direction, so I thought you might like to hear one-on-one why I have opted out.

Am I simply "missing it" with ACA? Am I to assume that the organization is hard at work for our benefit even though I can't recall my "counseling world" ever changing as a result of ACA's work? I am open to being enlightened. I "see" professionalism and results from my association with NBCC and CRCC, but not ACA. And the question of "What can I do to contribute to ACA?" has crossed my mind many times. Unfortunately, I know of no avenue into the organization to even offer my assistance, let alone having it accepted.

So I, being the good president that I was, responded:

Thanks for giving me an opportunity to reconvince you about your membership in the professional association of counseling. First, let me say that I am very sorry that you have chosen to not renew your membership in ACA. I have been a member of ACA since I was a graduate student in my MEd program, 30 years ago, and I have had my ups and downs too with ACA. I don't like everything that we do and I wish we were stronger societally, but I know that the only way to ever achieve our goals is by hanging together.

I want you to reframe your relationship to ACA—and it is a relationship. You wouldn't walk out on your wife or partner just because that person forgot to pickup your laundry, would you? How about because they had an incurable illness? How about if they had been nasty to you? How about if they were a Democrat and you were a Republican? Or they were a smoker and you were not? Or they were meeting some of your needs, but not every one? I hope you wouldn't. (Maybe on the smoker thing, I would.)

I also know that relationships work two ways. ACA has to give you something for you to care about us. If it's all negative, eventually you leave. If it's all positive all of the time, you definitely stay, but maybe you begin to take us for granted. If it's some negative and some positive and it's tilted more positive, you probably stay. It sounds to me from your message that you feel it's more negative now and you want to leave. It's your right. If we are not working hard to meet the needs of our profession and our professionals and if we are not being successful in meeting our goals and getting what we all need, then you ought to leave.

But remember it's hard to accomplish the survival of our profession in the world (I am willing to concede that maybe your personal goals are smaller than that). But that's why we band together in professional associations, so that our voices are more powerful. And that is what makes us have a stronger voice in global, national, state, and local issues—working together for the good of our profession and for the good of our clients. That's the big picture, Bill. It is critical that ACA survive so that our profession can survive and not become the handmaiden to LCSWs or psychologists or psychiatrists or . . . I'm sure you get my drift.

But see, by your action of not renewing and not belonging, you are insuring that we will never get what we have been working for and that we may in fact lose what we have already achieved. And you may unintentionally hurt yourself, our profession, and our society by your action.

I think that if you were around 100 years ago and saw the state of professional counseling or even just helping people who have problems, you would not be taking this action. You would see the worth of having a professional association that fights every day to maintain our historic gains and to move those gains even further. Looking back on the past 100 years, you would be able to see the significant progress that we have made as a profession. Mental health has not been highly regarded by policy makers. It is better now, but the change is incremental not revolutionary, and if you lose the professional associations that guard our benefits and progress, we all lose. And you think it is bleak out there now—wait until you see what happens when psychiatrists take over all mental health and education in our world.

I need to be blunt here—I think that you are being short-sighted. But in all fairness, we have to do our job too. Our public policy staff had the issue of Medicare coverage in our sights this year for the first time ever. We were so close. We have developed good relationships each year as we have gotten closer. And this year we were almost there, but if you leave and a bunch of others like you leave, we can't be as effective and get over the hump. Mental health parity is another one of those issues that we will get, but it is incremental. We have to change a lot of minds to get there. We had little control over the insurance industry, and I think that our insurance people did a great job under less than ideal instances. They are but human and this is all a human process and maybe we could have done more and better, but under the circumstances, we did as well as could be done, I assure you.

I'm also not going to go into a litany of all that you do get for your membership dollars (by the way, APA members pay over $300 a year). Come on, I know that you are disappointed, but we need all of us. I know that you care or you would not have called earlier and you would not be sending me this email. You want me to talk you out of this not-renewing-your-membership behavior. And that is what I am trying to do. I know that you are a fair person.

Answer this: Where do you think that NBCC, CACREP, CRCC, LPCs, the ethics code, funding for the Elementary and Secondary School Counseling Project, etc., came from? That is the past, but it is very relevant to your issues. What will ACA do in the future? It will be there to make sure that you have input into the standards revision and any of the new issues that spring up during our and others' lifetimes. Yes?

I hope you will reconsider. But no matter what happens, thanks for being a member for all these years. I appreciate that a lot.

Warmly, Mark

I got a reply in about a week:

Your last reply "hit a good nerve." The listing of ACA accomplishments were unknown to me. I knew the events/items existed, but I had no idea ACA was the driving force. I wonder how many others are ignorant as well? Maybe a "What We've Accomplished" article/mailing is in order.

Bottom line: I'll be renewing my membership next week.

Thanks for your time and interaction, Mark. I hope we're able to meet in person one day.

It's very gratifying personally and professionally when it all turns out this way.

This email exchange is a good example of why the "Big 4" (licensing, ethics, certification, and accreditation) are so very important. These "Big 4" for ACA and our members (and for any profession) assure a level of quality and adherence to professional standards—the behavioral norms of our profession. They assure a level of quality that others in society can count on. They assure that we will be here and that you will have a job doing the work that you were trained to do. They assure that you can help those who so desperately need our assistance.

Otherwise we'd all still be doing case management, like the vast majority (90%) of social workers are trained to do, or we would be assistants to psychologists or psychiatrists. Not that there's anything wrong with that, it's just that we are a different profession, trained to do counseling—whether personal or career—whether in schools, or agencies, or private practice—whether with individuals, or families, or groups—whether as guidance, or psychoeducation, or psychotherapy—whether we are diagnosing or assessing or testing—whether we are working on disciplinary issues or career issues or mental health issues or addictions or phobias or depression or whatever we have been appropriately trained to do by fully accredited programs that prepare us for licensing and certification and to be fully functioning and ethical members of the counseling profession.

I want to welcome you to our hardy band of professional counselors. Damn, we're good!

Reference

American Counseling Association. (2005). *ACA code of ethics*. Alexandria, VA: Author.

Chapter 16

The King Is Dead, Long Live the King

This is just me being humorous (this should be relatively familiar to you by now). This column is for Sam Gladding, Patricia Arredondo, and all the upcoming ACA Presidents who are reading this (you know who you are). It's my final column as your President. And I have quite mixed feelings about all of this.

On the one hand, I am sad to be stepping aside or down or over (some direction, actually, I guess it's more like "replaced"). It's been a good year in many ways. A lot has been accomplished (this is critical for us goal-oriented persons). You work for 20–30 years of your life to get to this point in your career and you get one shot to make a difference. There certainly were challenges at the beginning of this year, such as calls to revoke some divisions' charters, insurance carrier bankruptcy, general and divisional membership declines, a looming governance reorganization, and a tight budget. As I leave, no division charters were revoked and stronger intra-organizational ties have been forged, general and division memberships are once again on the increase, a financially successful convention and many other cost-saving measures made by staff have put us on track for a strong financial finish to our fiscal year, the governance reorganization issue was completed, and a new insurance carrier is now in place with a substantial history, secure and strong financial ratings, "occurrence" coverage, and less expensive rates. All in all, a very good year, all things considered.

On the other hand, I also find myself happy that it is over. It's not easy being ACA President, the leader of the largest professional counseling association in the world. In fact, this has been the hardest job I have ever had . . . and yet quite rewarding as well (I know there's a lesson in there somewhere). People treat you differently (that's both good and bad). People listen to every word you speak/write and they don't always hear it the way that you meant it. And you are on the road every week of your year—going somewhere, doing something.

At the beginning of the year, you are overwhelmed by the amount and quality of activity. By December, you are exhausted both physically and emotionally. Usually, ACA Presidents get sick during this time of the year. I never get sick (ask my partner Mario), but I got sick, real sick—twice during December with a fever and everything. Your immune system just gets run down.

I had a lot to do this year: planning and presiding over Governing Council meetings, Executive Committee meetings, COPARC meetings, and our first National Branch and Region Leadership Training Academy in Washington, DC.

And then there's the meetings that you do not have direct responsibility for but have to attend like the ACA Foundation, the ACA Insurance Trust, the Region business meetings, the standing committees and task forces of ACA, and many, many more.

Then there's the meetings with lawmakers on Capitol Hill and with the presidents and executive directors of our sister domestic and international professional associations (American Psychological Association, National Association of Social Workers, National Association of School Boards, National Association of Elementary School Principals, National Association of School Psychologists, National Education Association, American Federation of Teachers, British Association for Counselling and Psychotherapy, Canadian Counselling Association, and groups in Guam, Korea, China, Mexico, Turkey, and on and on).

Then comes the convention. It's the main event of your presidency in many ways. It's your chance to shine. If you do a good job, everyone remembers it. If you do a bad job, everyone remembers it. One shot. "Enjoy and revel in your convention" was the sage advice of Thelma Daley, our 24th ACA President (actually the American Personnel and Guidance Association then, but let's not quibble). The point from Dr. Daley was to stay in the moment and enjoy every little bit of this year and maintain perspective. (Please note that no one has ever chosen to be ACA President more than once.)

Now, I'm not trying to dissuade anyone from running for this position (really I'm not), but the loneliest time for me was when I was at our headquarters. You wouldn't think it would be lonely—what with the headquarters staff all around and the level of busy-ness all day long. But at night, when you go back to your hotel, no one is there that you know, except you. (Actually, you do get to know the hotel staff, but that doesn't count.) I rarely wanted to impose on the ACA staff to go and have dinner with me. They have done their work for the day and want to go to their homes and see their loved ones. There isn't a convention going on or another meeting of counselors and so you are not able to call up Jane Goodman or Judy Lewis and go have a drink and dinner together. When I was at our headquarters, I usually worked 12-hour days. And then called my partner Mario every night. I am now convinced that I can do anything for a year. (Smile.)

Anyway, based on my experiences this past year, here are my "Top Ten Rules of the Road for Future ACA Presidents." (Some are humorous and some are serious—you decide.)

1. When you meet strangers on the road, embrace them. You never know when you'll need a dinner companion.
2. Pay attention and focus on what you are doing at each moment, for example, a relatively simple behavior like dialing the telephone. On several occasions over the past year, I thought that I was dialing home when what I had actually dialed was the ACA headquarters telephone number. (This is very sad.)
3. Don't stand in the airplane seat with your shoes on. This is pet peeve of mine and has to do with the transfer of dirt from shoes to seat cushion. You never know who will be sitting there next, like someone in a pink chiffon prom dress.
4. Never take more than seven pairs of underwear, socks, or t-shirts in your luggage. Does the phrase "hotel laundry service" mean anything to you?
5. Pack light. At the end of a convention or conference or a big meeting, instead of carrying with you all of the Governing Council backup materials, books on Robert's Rules of Order, and sci-fi novels you have finished reading on your airplane trips, get a box from the hotel and ship your not-immediately-needed materials back home. That way, you'll also have lots of room in your luggage for the hotel amenities (shampoo, conditioner, mouth wash, etc.) that you have collected.
6. Busy doesn't always mean effective. There are always places you can go and things you can do, but you must learn to say no and focus your activity, so as to be congruent with your goals, or else you will not accomplish your vision.
7. Don't get bogged down in all of the details. Do the duties that are required: make decisions, handle crises, use your political skills to decide strategy and tactics, respond to questions and complaints, plan your convention, plan the governance meetings for which you have responsibility. But focus on the big picture. (This is a variation on #6 re: learning to say no.)
8. Honor and empower your governance and advisory groups. Touch them personally, individually, and humanely. You never know when you may want and need them to reciprocate.
9. Exhibit confidence, compassion, fairness, and patience at all times (but especially when presiding over the Governing Council meetings).
10. Stay in the moment. Love every minute of this experience, because there's nothing like it.

I have truly been blessed to have found our profession. I have been so honored to be your representative to the world this past year. I believe so very passionately in professional counseling, in the good that we do in the world. Freud talked about "love and work" as the hallmarks of the mature life. I count myself among the lucky ones in this world, for I have found what I love in my life—my partner Mario, my big inclusive family, my St. Francis

River Band of Cherokees, my friends, and you, my colleagues. Thank you for this—your acceptance, your respect, and yes, your love.

This is why I am here, involved with the American Counseling Association. Where else could a poor gay Cherokee boy from rural southeast Missouri grow up to be so honored, to be your President. Thank you for this important message to our students, our profession, and our world. I thank you from the bottom of my heart.

This final column is for Sam Gladding, Patricia Arredondo, and all the upcoming ACA Presidents. "Enjoy and revel" in your year as President, this is your time.

Note: This chapter was originally published as the "ACA President's Column" in the June 2004 issue of *Counseling Today*.

~~Chapter 17

And On an Even More Personal Note

I thought I'd throw this in at the end. It's like a *People Magazine* version of my life. Some of it was previously published in Bob Conyne and Fred Bemak's book, *Journeys to Professional Excellence: Lessons From Leading Counselor Educators and Practitioners* (Pope, 2005b) and in Jim Croteau, Julianne Lark, Melissa Lidderdale, and Barry Chung's book, *Deconstructing Heterosexism in the Counseling Professions: A Narrative Approach* (Pope, 2005a). Both offer more information on the lives of people in our profession, and I figure that since almost all of the people who will be reading this book and those other two are counselor types, counselor wannabes, or those-who-love-us, then you all might appreciate this chapter. It's about the influences on my life. It's poignant or illustrative or at least an easy read. I hope it touches you in some way. It's that Native American circle thing—you begin it with feelings, you end it with feelings. I hope you've enjoyed the journey.

Okay, so you've heard this mantra before if you've been reading this book thoroughly, but "I grew up as a poor gay Cherokee boy in rural southeast Missouri." I just love that line. It is so all-encompassing as a cultural identity tag. I tell you I'm putting it on a tombstone.

I tried to put all the leadership issues in the "10 (or so) Habits" chapter of this book (see Chapter 14), but I found as I was writing it that it was so objective, with little of my necessary subjective side, especially regarding how I have matured in the profession.

Here I want to talk about the more personal, individual mechanisms that have assisted me in my life. Generally, I have developed (ok, it took some work) a willingness to look at myself honestly and directly, an appreciation of the importance of congruence based on a sense of self, a strong personal and cultural identity, a knowledge of how I fit into the world, hope, a positive outlook, and the abilty to take responsibility for the part of my existence that I have some control over and knowing the difference. I also have developed a keen sense of humor. For me, an important way of surviving is humor. Humor is one of my personal qualities that is also most culturally derived—both from my Native American and gay experience — and that allows me to transcend feelings of anger and hurt. I have a rather dry intellectual wit that allows me to not take anything too seriously, especially myself, while always remaining passionately convinced that I am always right. See?

Also, as you have no doubt noticed, these narratives are filled with feelings. It was not always the case that I have had the power of my feelings available. I learned early the male role of hiding and denying my feelings— from others and myself. Through the process of being a client myself, I learned the power of reclaiming the awareness of my own feelings and ways to share them with others should I choose to. The first part of this was a battle at the personal level. The process of "coming out" is first and foremost a process of turning inward to battle your own personal, familial, cultural, and socially imposed demons. Further, when you have survived the death of the most important person in your life as I did when my partner of 13 years passed away in 1994, I have found that you can truly survive anything. Consciousness of self is the foundation upon which a true personal identity and then cultural identity are formed—first to recognize the feelings, acknowledge them honestly and directly, and then decide what to do with them.

I also want to acknowledge and further emphasize that few ever do any of this alone. I have had two magnificent partners in my life—Shahri, my partner who died, and now Mario, my love for the past ten years. Both supported and loved me with all of my good personal traits and all of my (shall we say) not so good ones—the image that comes to mind is "warts and all." Then there is my mother who always loves me unconditionally (she is an unconscious Rogerian); my grandmothers, both paternal and maternal; my three brothers, their partners, and my nieces and nephews who have taught me about the importance of patience and perspective; my teachers and counselors; my friends and sex partners. Finally, my mentors and my colleagues at work and in the counseling professions who have told me how great I am and also offered constructive feedback—both on an as-needed and regular basis.

I have actively sought these mentors, who have assisted and supported my work in the counseling professions. As I started making a list of those who have mentored me and had a profound effect on me and my career, I observed that many of them have been heterosexually oriented and mostly gay-positive. I had some, but few, formal or informal mentors who were sexual minorities. The major portion of that is the dearth of such individuals in the leadership of our profession.

In my work in the counseling professions, I know that there is a critical need for such mentoring, and I have actively tried to provide this for many people but especially for sexual minorities who were also racial/ethnic minorities in the USA—people like me. I carved out a specialty in career counseling for myself at a time when there were few who were practicing multicultural career counseling, especially sexual minority career counseling. In my counseling practice, I have actively sought such individuals as I recruited associates for my counseling and consulting firm as well as for leadership positions in the counseling professions. When others see that it is possible, they will come forward and we will now be there to help. The results of my elections to such positions will be felt throughout the counseling professions for years to come. Those of us who are multiculturalists in the broadest and most inclusive definition of the word are changing the face (truly) of our profession in profound ways.

I have always wanted to find a place for people like me in the counseling professions, and there were many years that it seemed there were none where I wanted to be. I and now many others are doing our best to change that in our profession.

I wrote in my second President's Column in the ACA newspaper, *Counseling Today* in August 2003, of the recent US Supreme Court decision that overturned the sodomy laws in the US. The headline of that column was "First We Were Sane, Now We Are Legal," and the first part of that headline refers to the removal in 1973 of homosexuality from the *Diagnostic and Statistical Manual of Mental Disorders (DSM)*. By a vote of the Board of Directors of the American Psychiatric Association, those of us who are gay, lesbian, or bisexual were made "sane" overnight. Wave your magic wand and you are no longer mentally ill. Get it? Do you understand the power we have to affect people's lives? We who are gay, lesbian, or bisexual were adjudged mentally ill because of the prejudices of the dominant culture. Let me repeat that, "We who are gay, lesbian, or bisexual were adjudged mentally ill because of the prejudices of the dominant culture." Nothing more, nothing less. We who are in the mental health professions have responsibility for that. That is why my election to lead one of the largest mental health organizations in the world is so important. As the first openly gay man elected to such a position, I represent a final and total repudiation of that past.

I broke through the lavender ceiling that existed in ACA for over 50 years and in NCDA for almost 90 years. Hopefully, it will not take an equal amount of time for the next sexual minority or Native American person to reach such positions.

References

Pope, M. (2005a). Crashing through the "lavender ceiling" in the leadership of the counseling professions. In J. M. Croteau, J. S. Lark, M. A. Lidderdale, & Y. B. Chung (Eds.), *Deconstructing heterosexism in the counseling professions: A narrative approach* (pp. 121–128). Thousand Oaks, CA: Sage.

Pope, M. (2005b). It takes a village to raise a leader: Meet Mark Pope. In R. K. Conyne & F. Bemak (Eds.), *Journeys to professional excellence: Lessons from leading counselor educators and practitioners* (pp. 197–216). Alexandria, VA: American Counseling Association.

Note: Portions of this chapter were originally presented as an invited lecture at Kent State University in Kent, Ohio, sponsored by their Chi Sigma Iota chapter in October 2003 (see Chapter 7), and as a presentation at the American Psychological Association Annual Convention in August, 2002, when I was elected as a Fellow.